First World War
and Army of Occupation
War Diary
France, Belgium and Germany

2 DIVISION
6 Infantry Brigade
King's Royal Rifle Corps
1st Battalion
12 August 1914 - 17 December 1915

WO95/1358/3

The Naval & Military Press Ltd
www.nmarchive.com
Published in association with The National Archives

Published by

The Naval & Military Press Ltd

Unit 10 Ridgewood Industrial Park,

Uckfield, East Sussex,

TN22 5QE England

Tel: +44 (0) 1825 749494

www.naval-military-press.com

www.nmarchive.com

This diary has been reprinted in facsimile from the original. Any imperfections are inevitably reproduced and the quality may fall short of modern type and cartographic standards.

© **Crown Copyright**
Images reproduced by permission of The National Archives, London, England, 2015.

Contents

Document type	Place/Title	Date From	Date To
Heading	WO95/1358/3		
Heading	1st Battalion King's Royal Rifle Corps Aug-Dec 1914		
Heading	6th Brigade 2nd Division 1st Battalion King's Royal Rifle Corps August 1914		
War Diary	1st Battalion The King's Royal Rifle Corps.	12/08/1914	31/08/1914
Heading	1st Battalion Kings Royal Rifle Corps. September. 1914		
War Diary	1st Battalion The King's Royal Rifle Corps.	01/09/1914	30/09/1914
War Diary	Diary	22/08/1914	26/08/1914
Heading	6th Brigade. 2nd Division. 1st Battalion King's Royal Rifle Corps October 1914		
War Diary	1st Battalion The King's Royal Rifle Corps.	01/10/1914	21/10/1914
War Diary	1st Battalion The King's Royal Rifle Cops.	01/10/1914	31/10/1914
Heading	6th Brigade. 2nd Division. 1st Battalion King's Royal Rifle Corps November 1914		
Miscellaneous	1st Battalion The King's Royal Rifle Corps. Novermber 1914	01/11/1914	18/11/1914
Miscellaneous	Casualties Officers 12 Aug-18th Nov		
Miscellaneous	Court Of Inquiry Reference Events 2nd November 1914 W Office Reference Events 2nd November Lt Office Reference 121/France/5568 K.R.R.C.		
Heading	6th Brigade 2nd Division. 1st Battalion King's Royal Rifle Corps December 1914		
War Diary	1st Battalion The King's Royal Rifle Corps.	04/12/1914	31/12/1914
Heading	2nd Division War Diary 1st Battn. Kings Royal Rifles January To June 1915		
Heading	1st Battalion The King's Royal Rifle Corps. January 1915		
War Diary	1st Battalion The King's Royal Rifle Corps.	01/01/1915	31/01/1915
Heading	6th Infantry Brigade. 2nd Division. War Diary 1st Battn. The King's Royal Rifle Corps. February 1915		
War Diary	1st Battn. The King's Royal Rifle Corps.	01/02/1915	28/02/1915
Miscellaneous	Reconnaissance Report Of 27.2.15 & Map.	27/02/1915	27/02/1915
Miscellaneous	Copy Of Report From 2nd Col Northey		
Diagram etc	Copy Of Rough Sketch Of Germany Trenches		
Heading	6th Infantry Brigade. 2nd Division War Diary 1st Battn. The King's Royal Rifle Corps. March 1915		
War Diary		01/03/1915	03/03/1915
War Diary	Copy Of 1/60th Diary.	02/03/1915	31/03/1915
Heading	6th Infantry Brigade. 2nd Division. 1st Battn. The King's Royal Rifle Corps. April 1915		
War Diary	Copy Of 1/60th Diary.	01/04/1915	30/04/1915
Heading	6th Infantry Brigade. 2nd Division. 1st Battalion King's Royal Rifle Corps. May 1915		
War Diary	Copy Of 1/60th Diary.	01/05/1915	31/05/1915
Heading	6th Infantry Brigade. 2nd Division. 1st Battn. King's Royal Rifle Corps. June 1915		
War Diary	1st Battn. The King's Royal Rifle Corps.	01/06/1915	30/06/1915
Heading	2nd Division War Diaries 1st Battn. Kings Royal Rifles. 1st July To 170819 December 1915		

Heading	6th Infantry Brigade. 2nd Division. 1st Battn. King's Royal Rifle Corps. July 1915		
War Diary	1st Battn. The King's Royal Rifle Corps.	01/07/1915	31/07/1915
War Diary	1/60th 6th Bde	29/07/1915	31/07/1915
Heading	6th Infantry Brigade. 2nd Division. 1st Battn. King's Royal Rifle Corps. August 1915		
War Diary	1st Battalion The King's Royal Rifle Corps.	01/08/1915	31/08/1915
Heading	6th Infantry Brigade. 2nd Division. 1st Battn. King's Royal Rifle Corps. September 1915		
War Diary	1st Battalion The King's Royal Rifle Corps. September 1915	01/09/1915	30/09/1915
War Diary		06/05/1915	07/05/1915
War Diary		28/09/1915	29/09/1915
Heading	1st Battn. The King's Royal Rifle Corps. October 1915		
War Diary	1st Battn. The King's Royal Rifle Corps. 1915	01/10/1915	31/10/1915
Heading	Report On Operations 3rd October.		
Miscellaneous	Report On Operations.	03/10/1915	03/10/1915
War Diary	1st Battalion, King's Royal Rifle Corps	01/10/1915	31/10/1915
Miscellaneous	DU		
War Diary	1st Battalion. King's Royal Rifle Corps. Appendix.	01/10/1915	31/10/1915
Heading	6th Infantry Brigade. 2nd Division. 1st Battn. The King's Royal Rifle Corps. November 1915		
War Diary	1st Battn. The King's Royal Rifle Corps. November 1915	01/11/1915	30/11/1915
Heading	6th Infantry Brigade. 2nd Division. Battn. transferred to 99th Bde. 2nd Div. 12.12.15 1st Battn. The King's Royal Rifle Corps. December 1915 1.12.15-17.12.15		
War Diary		01/12/1915	17/12/1915
Heading	1 Hants Regt Feb 1916 Vol XV C.h.g. Troops On Feb 20		

WO 95/13583/3

2ND DIVISION
6TH INFY BDE

1ST BATTALION
KING'S ROYAL RIFLE CORPS
AUG - DEC 1914

6th Brigade
2hd Division.

1st BATTALION

KING'S ROYAL RIFLE CORPS

AUGUST 1 9 1 4

1st Battalion The King's Royal Rifle Corps.

August 1914

(12/31.8.15)

12.8.14.

The Battalion left Salamanca Barracks, Aldershot, and entrained at Farnborough Station, A.and B.Corps at 5.50 a.m., C.and D.Corps at 6.50 a.m. A.and B.Corps arrived Southampton Docks about 8 a.m., C.and D.Corps at about 9 a.m. The Battalion embarked on S.S.Honorius and left Southampton about 12 noon. The ship anchored for an hour in Sandown Bay, I.W. for inspection by naval authorities and then proceeded to Havre, getting there about 12 midnight and, missing the tide, anchored for 12 hours.

13.8.14.

At 11 a.m., the tide being right, the ship proceeded up the Seine, reaching Rouen at 5.30 p.m. when the Battalion disembarked and marched to a rest camp just outside the town where they spent the night. (Mr.C.H.Wilkie appendicitis and to hospital for England).

14.8.14.

The Battalion entrained at Rouen at 8 p.m. The train left at about midnight and proceeded to Amiens which it reached at 5 a.m., 15.8.14.

15.8.14.

The train proceeded from Amiens via Arras, Cambrai, Busigny

to Vaux-Andigny, which was reached about 12 noon, where the Battalion detrained and proceeded by road to Hannappes via Mennevret and Tupigny. On reaching Hannappes at about 5 p.m. the Battalion at once went into billets, C.Coy. finding the in-lying Picquet for the night.

16.8.14.

The day was spent making all the arrangements re bounds, guards, rules to be observed while in billets, etc.

17.8.14. Route March -

The Battalion went for a route march at 9 a.m. via Vénérolles, Etreux, La Neuville and Iron, returning to Hannappes at 12 noon (about 6 miles).

18.8.14.

Route march Bhoeus d'en has, Etreux, Jerusalem (about 6 miles).

19.8.14.

Route march (about 6 miles).

20.8.14.

Route march (about 6 miles).

21.8.14.

Battalion left Hannappes 8.50 a.m. and marched to

Landrécies via Vénérolles, Etreux, Haute Rève, ~~which it reached~~ Arrived about 2.30 p.m, ~~On arrival~~ and went into billets in French Barracks for the night. (15 miles)

22.8.14.

Battalion left Landrécies at 5.30 a.m. and marched to Harguies via Maroilles, Noyelles, Leval, Pont-sur-Sambre, reaching Harguies 12.30 p.m. On arrival went into billets. B.Coy. supplied a picquet consisting of 1 platoon under Mr. Lloyd, which furnished 3 posts covering the western approaches to the village. A post of cyclists was also placed in the centre of Forêt de Mormal where 7 roads meet, 3 miles west of village. (14 miles)

23.8.14.

Battalion left Harguies 2.45 a.m. and marched to 4 miles north-east of Givry just short of Trieux via La Longueville, Riez de l'Erille, Gogmies, reaching Givry at about 11.30 a.m. (17 miles) At once proceeded to entrench. D.Coy, Capt.Lugard, furnished covering troops along railway embankment 2 miles north of Givry. C.Coy., Capt.Willan, entrenched along track running N.W. with right on main Givry road. On their left B.Coy., Capt.Maclachlan also entrenched. A Coy., Capt. Denison in reserve half a mile down main road towards Givry at Sugar Factory.

Enemy's artillery opened fire about 4 p.m. and searched the ground all round our artillery, kept up for about 1½ hours. A lot of fire round B. Company's trenches. Got a little sleep about 8.30 p.m. till 3 o'clock when enemy opened artillery fire again on our artillery, but not on infantry trenches. No casualties.

We left Trieux about 9 a.m. for Givry and then to Malplaquet at 1.20 p.m., where we rested till 3.45 a.m.

1 Rifleman of D Co missing from patrol North of TRIEUX.

24.8.14.

We moved to ½ N. of Bavai (15 miles), where we found Outposts. Major Lysons, Capt Bradford and Lieut Cavendish Bentinck joined.

25.8.14. German light force on our left as we moved out and through Bavai, 7.30 a.m. As rear guard on left of 6th I.B. we held on to Mecquegines, no opposition or advance by enemy, except that they occupied BAVAI directly we left it. Battn. then moved (through the Forest) de Mirbal to Pt.162 and thence and Pont sur SAMBRE via Aymeric 3.30 p.m. to Maroilles, Late and wet. 18 miles.

Turned out at 11 PM to support R.Berkshire Regt in attempt to capture Bridge West of village; Bridge not taken, but enemy prevented from crossing it. They had it barricaded and covered on a Field gun.

26.8.14. Retired as Rearguard to VENEROLLES via MARBAIX road and LE GRAND FAYT: met part of a French Reserve Division who were the first French troops we had actually seen.

27.8.14.
Right Flank guard to 6th I.B. moved at 9.25 through Hannapes, southwards to Mont D'Origuy. Bivouacked there for night 27th-28th: digging all night, on account of rumour of big German force near ST QUENTIN.

28.8.14.
via LA FERE
At 4.20 a.m. moved on southwards to Anigny, and with 2 long

4.

halts arrived there at 5.30 p.m.

28.8.14. ~~illegible~~

C.Coy. on duty at Bridge at Condren. A. B. and D. in billets in Avigny.

29.8.14.

Warned to be ready to move at about 6 a.m. to Bridge at Condren but later this was cancelled and we remained ready to move at short notice; a supposed rest day.

6 a.m. Left A{M}vigny (6th I.B.) after being ready to move since yesterday. Halted just S. {of village} till 9.15 a.m., passed through Barisis at 10 a.m. Very hot marching. Rond d'Orleans 10.50 a.m. Midday halt for dinners from 12 – 2 o'clock in Basse Forêt de Couchy, thence marched on and into bivouac at Couchy le Chateau at 6.15 p.m.

18/14
C-GA.

31.8.14.

Marched at 3 AM as rearguard to Bde, to SOISSONS.

~~Moved out at 5 a.m. southwards.~~

2 hours halt at Pommier at 12 o'clock, Moved on at 2 o'clock, C.Coy. as rearguard and arrived at St.Bandry about 4.30 p.m. C.Coy having remained behind (2 platoons as escort to Battery R.F.A. and 2 as R.G.) ~~(Bridge episode)~~. In Bivouac the B{attalion} was in reserve. 2 platoons C.Coy. and battery came in but the other 2 platoons stayed out till 12 mid. at the Bridge. Bridge was blown up at about 10.15 p.m.

1st BATTALION
KINGS ROYAL RIFLE CORPS.
SEPTEMBER, 1914

1st Battalion The King's Royal Rifle Corps.

September 1914

1.9.14.

Moved at 4 a.m. from St.Bandry towards south through Coeuvres (5.30 a.m.) Villers-Coteries where we had a halt for a meal at 10 o'clock; here the Guards Bde. who were rear guard and in an entrenched position about Soucy seemed to be in fairly close contact with the enemy; rifle fire being audible, and artillery fire being heavy (1 Battery with Rear Guard) The Bn. moved on forward before the duration of the halt was up and proceeded through the Forêt Domeniche de Retz. At the end of the Forêt we halted and about 4.30 p.m. were turned about and advanced to the N. edge of wood - B. on left, D. on right where our battery was in position and within 700^x of the Germans. No infantry was visible at this period. The Kings, Berks. and Staffords were in front or mixed with our 2 leading Coys.

C.Coy. went to the W.edge of the Forêt as escort to a battery of R.F.A. A.Coy. being in reserve. The enemy's artillery were firing along the edge of the wood where our infantry was holding the fence and bank (W).

We retired gradually through the wood about 5.30 p.m. None of the enemy following. The Cavalry Bde. covered the left flank

The enemy were apparently a mobile force which moved along in motors and were determined to do their worst in a short time. We had a long and tiring day and the bivouac at Thury was not reached till 9.30 p.m.

    Casualties: Lt. Masters, wounded (neck)
(no one killed)   N.C.O's and   Wounded 12.
    "   "   Missing 2ˣ

x 1 since returned.

2.9.14.

Left Bivouac at 4 a.m. 1st line transport preceded the Battalion. Passed through Betz at 5.40 a.m. and thence moved southwards, 5th Bde. following the 6th and Guard Bde. being ahead. ~~11.30 a.m. passed Entrepilly. Hottest day to march we have had as yet. Halt for 1 hour at Montceaux, then moved on through Pierre-Levee to B~~Barbeaux-les-~~Taunes (3 miles south of Pierre-Levee, where we~~ arrived about 2.30 p.m. and halted for the night. Very long & hot march — (at LA CONGÉ FARM near TRILBARDOU)

14. Marched at 2 AM via MEAUX, TRILPORT — MONTCEAUX, and PIERRE LEVEE to BILBARTEAUX FARM, where we bivouacked in a stubble field.

9.14 — Troops had a good night's rest and breakfast about 7 o'ck. a.m. The Brigade received orders to resume march south-west about 3.30 p.m. The Battalion was in rear of 6th Bde. Very warm. Halted at 4.30 p.m. for remainder of Div. to pass. Arrived in Bivouac at Voisins at 6.30 p.m. Very slow march.

1st Reinforcement; 2nd Lt. Saltmarshe and 99 others, arrived.

~~(one platoon on outposts side).~~

5.9.14.

Left again at 2.50 a.m. via Tre~~fmes~~ SN -Faremoutiers ~~Forêt~~, FORÊT-de-Crecy, ~~Lumigny~~ LUMIGNY Arrived at 6.15 a.m. Passed large numbers of Refugees en route. Cool march, but troops did not have breakfast before leaving. Arrived at Chaumes at 11 a.m. (about 22 miles). We remained there in *bivouack* for the night 4th-5th September. Not very nice but cool. Furthest point south reached; *end of retirement which had lasted since 24th August, during which time we hardly ever got into a bivouack before dark, and almost always started before daylight*

6.9.14.

Enemy retiring. Marched at 6.30 a.m. northwards from Cha~~nines~~umy to Cha~~b~~uisson Farm, where 6th Bde. was in Reserve to 1st Corps (arrived 8 a.m.). Remained there till 6.20 p.m., then we marched to Chateau la Fo^Ntelle, arriving at 7.25 p.m., ~~they~~ where we bivouacked for the night in a stubble field. Warmer than last night.

7.9.14.

Moved at 9.45 a.m. up the road into the shade of a wood ($\frac{1}{4}$ mile). Moved on again at 4.30 p.m. to just S.W. of St.Simeon, where we arrived at 7.15 p.m. and bivouacked for the night in a stubble field.

8.9.14.

Left at 8 a.m., marching towards Charly via Rebais. (Bn. was in rear of 6th F.B.) and in rear of Division. Heard that the V. French army had had a very successful day yesterday on our right, taking 1200 prisoners, also VI. French army did very well on our left. Our Cavalry in a small force was very successful against the German rear-guard in superior numbers, the latter retiring fast before the 18th Hussars and 9th Lancers.

Capt.Makins and Lt.Wakefield-Saunders with 2 N.C.O's and 98 others joined the Bn. on evening of 7th at the bivouac and this made the Bn. about 1130 strong. Makins to command of A. Coy. and Saunders to D.Coy.

Passed through Rebais at 11.50 a.m. Enemy now reported in position near La Tretoire (small and tired rear-guard) which was pushed back and our artillery opened fire on their transport which was passing westwards along the valley of the R.Marne. Enemy reported to be in position on hills round Boitron, force unknown at present (1 p.m.)

Our artillery firing from ¾ mile south of Champ-la-Bride 2 p.m. Column in front of us moved forward, including transport and mechanical. We moved on at 4.50 through La Tretoire and over the River Morin and up the opposite side of the valley a very steep hill indeed and all covered with woods and high banks which afforded good cover to the enemy to fire at our artillery advancing down the south slope to the river.

Arrived in bivouac at La Noue about 8 p.m., and Bde. took up a line behind woods facing R.Maine.

9.9.14.

Bde. moved on at 4.30 a.m. round E. of wood. in front of bivouac, advanced on river bridge at Charly which was barricaded and took two hours to clear, crossed bridge at 8.15 a.m. C. A. D. B. in order of march to occupy hills on opposite, N. side.

9.0 a.m. C. Coy reached summit of hill, N. of Charly. Inhabitants reported that the majority of the enemy left the village last night: just a small party of cyclists hung on to the N. side of bridge.

Halted here for 7 hours and moved on at 4 p.m. due North via Villiers to Domptin (5 p.m.), arrived in bivouac at Coupru at 6 p.m.

10.9.14.

Left Coupru at 4 a.m., moving north via Mariguy.

Battn. with Berks as vanguard and 50th Battery R.F.A., on arriving at south end of village of HAUTES VESNES a column of the enemy was reported marching up road from

Vierly to Chezy en Orxois. The 50th Batty. R.F.A. were immediately brought up, and opened fire on enemy in force at 1500^X from S.W. edge of Hautvesnes.

Enemy then lined the side of the road which at this point ran through a cutting forming a natural trench. C.Coy. were ordered to attack, starting with their left on the right of 50th Batty., and advanced across an open stubble field to a position about 400^X in front of the guns on the forward slope of the hill. B.Coy. were sent round by N. side of village under cover of a Sunken Lane, and then reinforced C. Coy's right and centre. A. Coy. was deployed on left of C. Coy. and D. Coy. kept in reserve in a Sunken Lane until another Batt. was deployed on our right.

As soon as our guns opened fire the enemy brought 4 guns into action from high ground just N. of Brennatz, at the same time our own guns opened by mistake on the Hd.Qrs. of the Batt. from a S.W. direction. Fire coming from this direction enfiladed the road, and one shell bursting by Hd.Qrs. wounded Lt. Woods *and Adjutant*, Sgt.Richardson (Sig.) L/Cpl.Willows (Cyclist) and Rfn.Butler (groom). *2 Coy S Staffords came up eventually on our left and 2 Coy of Kings on our Right. Berkshire Regt remained N.E of village watching our Right Flank*

Fire of our guns and heavy rifle fire of the Batt. silenced the enemy, who eventually after 1½ hours fighting put up white flags and surrendered; *they had about 80 killed and wounded and we took 450 prisoners; about 500 of them got away toward CHEZY but were captured by the 3rd Division; enemy Passe↑ away.*

We had the following casualties:

10 NCOs & Riflemen killed
4 Officers and 60 others wounded
5 Riflemen missing -

1 platoon of B. Coy. left as escort to prisoners. ~~We took between 450 and 500 prisoners~~. We bivouacked at Chevillon.

11.9.14.

Left bivouac at 5 a.m. B.Coy. still with prisoners. Marched via Latelly where we halted for about 1 hour from 8 to 9 a.m. Halted again in Breing and eventually got to billets at Wallée about 4.30 p.m. in heavy rain.

12.9.14.

Left billets at 5.45 a.m., marched without incident to Mont Hussard Farm, which we reached about 8 p.m., in an awful rain storm. We halted for an hour about 1 mile N. of Braine to get supplies and bury Germans. MONT HUSSARD FARM where the Brigade spent the night had accomodation for about 1 Battalion: everybody was drenched to the skin.

13.9.14.

Left billet about 5 a.m., marched about 2 miles and rested for 9 hours in a stubble field. Very cold. Bradford wounded in foot by own revolver. Reached billets at Dhuiseh about 6.30 p.m. Comfortable billets.

14.9.14.

Left billets at 3.30 a.m., marched via Pont D'Arcy over pontoon bridge to Verneuil, where Batt. was split up, C. and B. Coys. under Capt. Willan were sent out to the right to get touch with 5th Bd. and A. and D. Coy. under Major Armitage to the left to La Burette Wood to get touch with Guards Brigade.

(A. and D. Coys.) were shelled crossing open ground from Canal until under cover of wood. A few men were hit by shrapnel. Eventually got in touch with Guards by road running N. from Soupir, were sniped at by enemy. Immediately deployed to drive out Germans, but meanwhile more Guards came up and owing to tactics of snipers suffered several casualties. We then reformed half way down the wood, Rifles on right and Irish Guards on our left. Advanced straight through wood driving enemy out on far side and inflicted considerable loss on them as they retired. ~~We had the following casualties:~~

As we were lining the edge of the wood we were shelled by our own guns as well as the enemy's. G.Makins was wounded at this time.

The Irish Guards then withdrew to position half way down wood. We maintained our position on edge of wood until dusk, when we received orders from 2nd Division to say we were to conform with the movements of the Guards Bde. We therefore withdrew and prolonged the right of the Irish Guards, leaving posts out in front.

15.9.14.

At dawn we again advanced to edge of wood and entrenched with entrenching tools, picks or shovels available. Our right at this time was exposed owing to the position being too extended for the men we had.

During the day a Coy. of Berks came up to the wood in rear of is. We were under shell fire all day and unable to light fires.

16.9.14.

A Coy. of the Berkshires came up and prolonged our right taking over our position in the quarries. Later on a Coy. of the Oxfords was sent up to support us during the night with order to make an attack on enemy's left. Owing to this Coy.

not knowing the ground and darkness coming on, Lt.Saunders and 20 N.C.O's and men undertook this task and went out at 11.30 p.m. and fired on enemy's trenches. The enemy replied, but fired towards our left. Saunders' party got back without any casualties.

17.9.14.

The Oxford Coy. was withdrawn from us and sent to relieve the Grenadier Guards, who were on the left of the line. We fired on the enemy's observation post on the haystacks.

18.9.14.

Usual shelling and sniping.

19.9.14.

About 2 p.m. enemy commenced shelling much more vigorously than usual and a regular attack began on the whole line. The enemy's infantry then advanced and brought up machine guns. Alston was wounded early, Rankin looking after Alston had his leg shattered by a shell from our own guns, Armytage being hit a quarter of an hour later by another shell, but escaped with only a bruise.

The enemy's infantry attack was only half hearted and after dark they could be heard close by, but made no further attack.

Good work was done by Rfn. Bullock and Baker, who kept up observation from the top of a tree during shell fire.

20.9.14.

About 2 a.m. on the 20th B. and C. Coy., with Hd.Qrs. came up to our support and relieved us in the trenches at 4.30 a.m.

A. and D. Coys. then went down to Soupir, where we rested till 4.30 in the afternoon. B. and C. Coys. were relieved by the S.Staffords and the Battn. marched to billets. A. and D. Coys. going to Verneuil and B. and C. and Hd.Qrs. to Moussy, arriving there about 8 p.m.

~~The following casualties occurred during the week.~~

14.9.14.

B. and C. Coys. Right flank Guard were heavily attacked in front by infantry in flank by machine guns in wood about 700^X N. of Tilleul. These 2 Coys. put up a very good fight and killed a large number of the enemy before retiring to Tilleul, where they were reinforced by Companies of the Worcester and H.L.I. Capt. Maclachlan, Lt.Lloyd and Co.St. Major of B.Coy. were all hit. Here as later with A. and D. Capt. Rankin. R.H.P.K. did splendid work, as also did Lt.Lloyd who when wounded himself and out between English and German fire collected the other wounded into a place of safety.

Night of 14-15.9.14.

This $\frac{1}{2}$ Battn. under Lt.Col.Northey, advanced to Tilleul de Courtelan and then W. to Malval where instead of the 6th Bde. Hd.Qrs. they tumbled into a mass of Germans collecting near a large Signal lamp. At midnight, in conjunction with 5th Bde. we retired back to Verneuil.

17-19.9.14.

On 17th to 19th this $\frac{1}{2}$ Battn. was in Reserve at Verneuil on night of 19th-20th reinforced A. and D. Coys. in trenches above Soupir.

Total casualties, 14th to 21st:

Officers wounded:

    Capt. Maclachlan.

    Capt. Makins.

    Lieut. Alston.

    Lieut. Lloyd.

    Lieut. Bentick.

Others: 27 Killed.

    136 wounded.

    18 missing.

<u>21.9.14</u>.

Rested in our billets all day and moved to Oeuilly during the night, arriving there about 4 a.m.

Lt. Waring and 3rd reinforcements joined.

<u>22-23-24.9.14</u>.

Rested at Oeuilly and refitted, new shirts, etc.

G.O.C. 2nd Divn. visited and congratulated Battn. on work done.

Col. Fanshawe took over command of Brigade from General Davies, who had been ill for some days.

(We were close to 2nd Battn. and saw several of them).

25.9.14.

Left Oeuilly about 2 o.m. for Bourg, relieving S.Staffords who were sent to Soupir.

C.Coy. was out on the hill during the night.

Haig and Maynard arrived.

26.9.14.

Left Bourg at 6.30 p.m. to relieve Cameron Highlanders in trenches N. of Verneuil. C.Coy. in valley N. of Beaune with a platoon.

27.9.14.

Half hearted attack on trenches about 7 p.m. Lt.Col. Northey and 3 Rfn. wounded. Hd.Qrs. and D.Coy. as support moved down to Verneuil about 10.30 p.m. and went into billets there.

28.9.14.

Our new machine gun took up position by new observation post on top of A. and B. Coys' cave and opened fore on enemy's trench. Enemy's horse battery opened on it at 1600^X. Lt. Brocklehurst was wounded about 12.30 p.m. and water jacket punctured by shrapnel. Lt.Gough took over command of B.Coy. L/Cpl. of C. Coy. killed by sniper.

29.9.14.

Everything quiet till about 3 p.m., when enemy's horse gun opened on trenches. 3 Rfn. killed and 11 wounded by third shell.

C. Coy. in Beaune heavily shelled. One Rfn. A. Coy. attached platoon wounded.

D. Coy. relieved B. Coy. in cave trenches.

30.9.14.

Rfn. killed by expanding bullet, 1 Rfn. wounded by ditto. Usual shelling took place.

DIARY.

22ᵈ Sept. 2.30 a.m. Brigade moved from MOUSSY and VERNEUIL to billets in OEUILLY as reserve to 1ˢᵗ Army arriving about 4 a.m.

23ᵈ. Brigade rested at OEUILLY. General Munro visited the battalions' billets.

24ᵗʰ. ditto. Lt Col. Serocold and some of the Officers 2ⁿᵈ Battalion came down to see us.

25ᵗʰ. 8.10 a.m. Battalion were warned that it would be required in the evening to relieve 1ˢᵗ Brigade in firing line. This order later cancelled. Battalion ordered to move at 2 p.m. to BOURG. Arrived there 3 p.m. and went into billets. "C" Company sent to northern end of ridge just north of BOURG where they remained the night without incident and were recalled at daybreak 26ᵗʰ. In the evening Major R. Haig, 6ᵗʰ R.B. joined for attachment and took over transport from Lieut. Gough. Lieut. Maynard joined (posted to "D" Coy.).

26ᵗʰ. Brigade ordered to relieve 1ˢᵗ Brigade in trenches. Battalion ordered to move to VERNEUIL at 6.30 p.m. Battalion left VERNEUIL 8 p.m. and took over trenches near Cave on BEAULNE spur from Camerons during night. "C" Company being in valley west of BEAULNE with platoon of "A" Company

6th Brigade.
2nd Division.

1st BATTALION

KING'S ROYAL RIFLE CORPS

OCTOBER 1914

1st Battalion The King's Royal Rifle Corps.

October 1914

1.10.14.

    Battn. left Verneuil about 11.30 p.m. and took place of S.Staffords, who had been in support of Rifle Brigade at Rifleman's Point, Staffords taking over their trenches. B. and D. Coys' close behind Staffords' trenches. Hd.Qrs., A. and C. Coy. in wood at La Bovette. No casualties.

2.10.14.

    Move above mentioned completed about 3 a.m. Battn. rested all day.

3.10.14.

    Battn. rested all day.

4.10.14.

Battn. paraded at 7 p.m. and relieved S.Staffords at Rifleman's Point.

5.10.14.

2 a.m. 4th Reinforcements arrived.

Capt. Beauchamp Seymour to B. Coy.
" Lynes " D. "
Lieut. Sweeting " B. "
" Clowes " C. "

also 69 N.C.O's and Rfn.

About 11 a.m. German guns started shelling B. Coys. trenches and Gunners' Observation post. One man killed and 3 wounded.

6.10.14.

Battn. had a pretty quiet day at Fifleman's Point. improving their trenches and communications through wood in rear of their trenches.

No casualties.

7.10.14.

Quiet day except enemy's artillery more active. In evening C. Coy. sent out a patrol into wood in their front to draw enemy's fire and endeavour to discover his strength.

Moon too bright for them to get far.

8.10.14.

About 3 a.m two patrols were sent out by A. Coy. to draw enemy's fire. They could only advance a few yards owing to moonlight and had one man slightly wounded. Lt. Clowes and 2 Rfn. wounded.

About 11 p.m. Capt. Willis, 5th Battn., and 2nd Lieut. Reynard, Capt. Wells Ward and Cronk arrived. Lieut. Bourke returned to Battn.

Wells, A. Coy., Ward to C. Coy., Willis to B. Coy., and Cronk to D. Coy.

9.10.14.

Quiet day - 3 wounded.

10.10.14.

Quiet day - 5 wounded.

11.10.14.

Quiet day. Prepared to hand over to Kings' 5 p.m. Relief cancelled.

12.10.14.

Fairly quiet day. Horse artillery gun rather troublesome. Rfn. Hubbard killed. Berks fired hay stacks which drew enemy's fire about 9 p.m.

13.10.14.

H.A. Gun shelled us in the morning. L/Cpl.Wadner wounded. Relieved by French about 1 a.m.

14.10.14.

Marched to Oeuilly 7 a.m. Shelled. 2nd shell killed Baker about 1 a.m. (C.O's servant) and 1 man, 2nd Battn. wounded, Harman and 4 others.

15.10.14.

Marched to Bazoches, 4 a.m. Rested there all day. At 10 p.m. marched to Fesmes and entrained at midnight, destination unknown.

16.10.14.

At 3.22 a.m. train left Fesmes. (Passed through Amiens and Boulogne.)

17.10.14.

Detrained at Strazeele. Marched at 1.10 p.m. to Hazebrouck and went into billets at 3 p.m. Major Armytage went sick, and Captain Willan assumed command of the Battn.

18.10.14.

The Battn. spent the day in the same billets.

19.10.14.

Still at Hazebrouck. A party of 38 Riflemen, some of the fifth reinforcements, arrived, also Captain Llewellyn and Lieutenant Birkett joined for duty with the Battn. Suddenly received orders to move and left at 3.30 p.m. for Godewaersvelde, where we arrived at 7.30 p.m. and went into billets.

20.10.14.

The Brigade marched at 6.30 a.m. and the Battn. went into billets at Ypres.

21.10.14.

Left Ypres at 5 a.m.

1st Battalion The King's Royal Rifle Corps.

October 1914

Oct.
1st. Battalion left VERNEUIL about 11.30p.m. and took place of South Staffords who had been in support of 3rd Rifle Brigade at Rifleman Point - Staffords taking over their trenches. H.Qs, "A" and "C" in wood at LA BOVETTE.

2nd. Move above mentioned completed about 2 A.M. Battalion rested all day.

3rd. Battalion rested and slept night in bivouac at LA BOVETTE.

4th. Battalion paraded at 7 p.m. and relieved South Staffords at "Rifle Point".

5th. 2 a.m. 4th Re-inforcement arrived.
Capt. Beauchamp Seymour to "B" Company.
 "   W. Lynes.   D   "
Lieut. H.C Sweeting   B   "
 "   C.G.E Clowes   C   "
Also 69 N.C.Os and Riflemen.
About 11a.m. German guns started shelling "B Company's" trenches and Gunners observation post. Tony Musters R.F.A was I'm afraid very badly hit by shell in back of head. Also 1 Man killed and 4 wounded. (and 2 men of R.F.A).

6th. Battalion had a pretty quiet day at Rifleman's point. Improving their trenches and communications through wood in rear of their trenches. Returned a 'nil' casualty return.

OCT.
7th. Quiet day, except enemys' artillery rather more active. In evening "C" Company sent out patrol into wood to their front to draw enemys fire and endeavour to discover his strength. The moonlight was too bright for them to get far.

8th. About 3 a.m 2 patrols were sent out by "A" Company to draw enemys' fire, they could only advance a few yards owing to moonlight, and had one man slightly wounded. During the day 2/Lieut. Clowes and 2 men were wounded by high explosive shrapnel. They were digging in a trench on the forward slope of "Rifle Mound" and were suddenly fired on by enemys' battery near BRAYE. About 11 p.m the following Officers turned up.
Captain A.L.Y. Willes. 5th Bn.
Lieut. C.H. Reynard (regular officer) 2nd Bn
Captain W.H. Wells 5th Bn
" H.E. Ward } Spl. Res. 3rd Buffs.
Lieut. G. Cronk
and Lieut. E.G.W. Bourke returned from Hospital.

9th. Quiet day. Nights are getting very cold. Our principal amusement by day is to watch our artillery fire and help the gunner officer to observe.
Casualties - 3 Riflemen wounded.

Oct.
10th. Another quiet day.
Casualties 5 Riflemen wounded (1 accidentally)

11th. Prepared to hand over to King's Regt. but relief cancelled at last moment.
10 p.m. sent our blankets away to blanket wagons so spent a very cold night.
Casualties for day Nil.

12th. Very quiet day. Hot sun very pleasant after cold night. Lieut. H.C. Maynard re-joined from hospital.
Heard that Col. Northey was at ROUEN and going on well - bullet extracted.
Sgt. Major Beck not very well.
Casualties - 1 Rfn. Killed.
About 9 p.m. the Berks on our right sent out a patrol which set fire to some hay stacks near the canal near BEHYE, this stirred up the Germans who did a lot of rifle shooting opposite our right Company "C" and also the German H. Artillery battery (supposed to be about 500 yards north of our trenches). The latter broke a rifle in "A" Company and knocked two sword bayonets off rifles in "C" Company, but we had no casualties.
After half an hour the firing died away. The Germans threw a good many light bombs over us.

Oct
13th. During the morning 2/Cpl. now 2/Lieut. S. Wadner "C" Company was wounded by a shell from the H.A. Battery. At 7 p.m. we were told that we were to be relieved by 38th Regiment of Chasseurs about 9 p.m. The latter did not however turn up till after 1 a.m.

14th The relief went off quietly.
The Companies marched independently down to SOUPIR and then we moved by half battalions into our old billets in ŒUILLY.
Very glad to get a roof over our heads again as during the march we had some heavy rain. We got into billets about 6 a.m. Had a good hot bath, the first I had for ages. Was just (about 11 a.m) lying down to get a sleep when two "coal boxes" came down in quick succession within a few yards of our Headquarters and Mess. The second burst just outside the gate, broke all our windows and covered us with dust, killed 2 men, wounded three including the Quartermaster (Harman) and slightly wounded the sentry on the gate.

15th. 4 a.m. Brigade left ŒUILLY. Battalion followed King's Regiment and marched via VILLERS and PERLES to BAZOCHES.

OCT.
had a good deal of trouble with transport of other Units which kept getting in the way. Roads very greasy and steady rain all the way.
Arrived BAZOCHES 9 a.m.
10 p.m. marched from BAZOCHES and entrained at FISMES 12 midnight. [Whole battalion in one train except 100 men of 'A' Company under Lieut. C.V.H. Gough who followed with Brigade Headquarter train]

16th. 3.22 a.m. train left FISMES [and went via MAREUIL SUR OURCQ, ORMOY - LA PLANIE, ST. DENIS - AMIENS - ETAPLES - BOULOGNE - (left 5 a.m.)

17th. CALAIS - left CALAIS 9.20 a.m. went via ST. OMER and] detrained at STRAZEELE. Marched from latter 1.10 p.m. and arrived at HAZEBROUCK at 3 p.m. and went into billets there. Major G.A. Armytage went sick and Captain F.G. Willan took command of the Battalion.

18th. Brigade spent all day in billets at HAZEBROUCK spent all day taking summaries of evidence and at Court martial. Very good shops at HAZEBROUCK and not looted at all by Germans.

19th. About 2 a.m. party of 38 Riflemen joined. Capt. W.D. Llewellyn and 2nd Lieut. C.E.G. Birkett, 3rd Somersets. S.R. joined on attachment.

Oct.

At 3-15 p.m. Brigade suddenly received orders to move. Battalion left HAZEBROUCK at 4.30 p.m. and marched via ST. SYLVESTRE and EECKE to GODEWAERSVELDE where the Brigade went into billets about 7.30 p.m.

20th. The Division marched at 6 a.m. 4th Brigade forming advance guard, 5th Brigade left flank guard. The Battalion (3rd in Brigade) left GODEWAERSVELDE at 6.30 a.m. and marched via BOESCHEPE — RENINGHELST to YPRES and billeted on northern outskirts of YPRES. Headquarters and 2 Companies being in the lunatic asylum. Very comfortable bed, also men very nice attics full of straw above asylum. Lunatics harmless, dangerous ones locked up!!

21st. 5 a.m. Brigade left YPRES and moved to WIELTJE, as reserve brigade to Division which was ordered to attack in direction of PASCHENDALE 4th Brigade being in front on right and 5th Brigade on left. Battalion spent day in support of other two Brigades on WIELTJE – PASCHENDALE road about 1 mile N.E. of former. [We could hear a good deal of shelling and rifle fire going on especially to our right, but no shells came near us] We had our Heavy Battery about 100 yds behind us who fired steadily all day [and kept us awake!]

Oct.
About 8 p.m. we returned to ST. JEAN and went into billets for the night

22nd. [Routine Orders arrived the following] N.C.O's granted commissions as 2nd Lieuts. dated 11th October:-

Coy Sgt Maj. C. S. Schoon.   LSgt. S. Lucas.
   "   R. Richards.   "   C. Collins.
Sergt.   J. Casey.   Corpl. T. Wadner.
   "   R. H. Slater.   LCpl. F. Wadner.
LCpl.   K. H. W. Ward (enlisted day we left Aldershot)

About 4 p.m. Battalion and Kings Regt. suddenly ordered off. Marched (following Kings) via POTIJZE and ZILLEBEKE to KLEIN ZILLEBEKE where we bivouacked in a field - ready to support 3rd Cavalry Division who were expecting a heavy attack.

About 9 p.m. there was a lot of heavy rifle fire in the direction of the cavalry trenches of these three Brigades especially to our right and we were ordered to fall in on the road. After about an hour however, firing having died away, we returned to our bivouac. Willan and I slept in Brigade Headquarters (a public house). (reference OSTEND map).

23rd. At 3 a.m. Battalion moved back to its old billets in ST. JEAN as Corps reserve - arriving 5 a.m. (ST. JEAN is 1½ miles N.E. of YPRES).

| Oct. | About 10 a.m. suddenly ordered to move off to farm about 1 mile S.E. of PILKEM in support of 1st Division and under their orders. About 3 p.m. 'A' and 'D' Companies moved from our Headquarters at farm to 1st Brigade (General Fitz Clarence) Headquarters and remained under his orders until 7.30 a.m. 24th. Headquarters and remaining two companies stayed at Farm till about 6 p.m. when they moved into billets at PILKEM - very dirty billets. |
| 24th | 12.15 a.m. 'B' Company sent up about 600 yards north of PILKEM to block road and be in support of Queen's Regiment. This Company re-joined Headquarters about 8 a.m. and 'A' and 'D' Companies re-joined about an hour later. Battalion thus all together at PILKEM. At 2.30 p.m. Battalion was ordered to re-join 6th Bde. whose Head quarters were on the EKSTERNEST - ZONNEBEKE road. Battalion marched 3 p.m. via POTIJZE and FREZENBERG and went into billets near Brigade Headquarters about 8 p.m. The Battalion and South Staffords being in support of Berks and King's Regt. [On arrival we heard that Col. Bannatyne (King's Regt) had been killed during the afternoon attack of 6th Brigade on portion of ridge |

Oct.
just S.E. of ZONNEBEKE. I slept in Bde. Headquarters. "B" Company had one man killed by a "Spent" bullet on the way to their billets close to Bde. H. Qrs. and a horse was killed just outside the door of the latter during the night.

25th Our Brigadier (General Fanshawe) was very slightly grazed on knee also by a Spent bullet about 12 noon - about 200 yds. from his H. Qrs.

2nd Division did not move till 3 p.m. as it was necessary to wait until the French 18th Corps came past the left of 6th Brigade near cross roads on ridge just East of ZONNEBEKE.

Battalion and South Staffords forming 6th Brigade reserve moved off from their billets about 4 p.m. and advanced along northern edge of big wood west of REUTEL and bivouacked in a farm just north of junction of 5 tracks on edge of this POLYGONE Wood. There was a lot of rifle fire in the wood on our right during the evening and also the night and there was a good deal of artillery fire all day.

Officers billeted in and round farm. Rained all ~~during~~ night.

Oct. 26th 3.30 a.m. verbal orders were given to C.O. as follows — Battalion was to fill a gap between right of King's Regt. and Irish Guards. This gap he was told would occur as King's and Irish Guards advanced. There was not much time to give detailed instructions to companies as it was getting light and there was no time to get in touch with Irish Guards and find out exactly where their left rested. 'D' Company advanced first followed by 'C' Company, 'A' and 'B' being in support for the time being. At 5.30 a.m. when 'D' Company joined up with right of King's Regt. it was just light enough to make out objects at 300 or 400 yards. As soon as 'D' Company got clear of the edge of the wood (100 yds or so into the open) they came under a very heavy enfilade fire from rifles and two machine guns on their left which they were unable to locate at the time but which were probably in a house. They were quite unable to advance. The left of 'D' Company with whom was Capt. Lynes got into some old (French?) trenches in a turnip field and the right of the Company were quite unable to move.

2nd Lieut. Ward's platoon had to dig themselves in as they lay in the turnips.

Lieut. Saunders got his into the edge of the wood where they suffered severely from enfilade fire – 2nd Lieut Cronk (Buffs. S.R. attached) was killed on the right. – apparently he was under the impression that the Germans were retiring out of their trenches and rushed forward with part of his platoon. The Germans allowed them to get well out into the open and then opened a very heavy fire. Almost all this party were either killed or wounded.

The two leading Companies maintained their positions all day while 'A' and 'B' remained in reserve in a fir wood about 300 yards in rear. The latter Companies had a few men hit by the stray bullets which came past all day. ~~At dark we improved our trenches~~.

During the morning as it was discovered that there was a considerable gap between the right of 'D' Company and the left of the Irish Guards. 'C' Company were sent up to fill it.

During the afternoon the two supporting Companies were taken away to act as support to left of Brigade but did not come into action. In the afternoon I was sent to look for the Headquarters

OCT.

of the Irish Guards with whom we were to co-operate with a view to an advance. I rather overshot the mark and nearly walked calmly up to a German trench which was much more forward than our information led us to believe. During the day the Battalion lost 47 casualties – 13 Killed 34 wounded, including 1 Officer Killed (2nd Lieut. G. Cronk. 3rd Buffs. attached) and two Officers wounded [2nd Lt. R.H. Ward and Lieut. E.G.W. Bourke]. Nearly all the casualties occurred in 'D' Company, but there were some in 'C' and 3 or 4 in the supporting companies also. The Battalion remained in position all night and improved trenches, but were relieved by the Irish Guards about

27th. 5 a.m. and went down to a farm in the valley south of ZONNEBEKE where we had breakfast. 'C' and 'D' Coys. found the other two companies already at this farm when they arrived.

About 9 a.m. Battalion was ordered to advance on left of the Staffords and keeping touch with the French on their left. 'A' Company led off at once and was shortly followed by 'B' in support. The other half Battn. being kept in reserve temporarily where they were. The Staffords were to

advance with their left on a small road
running South west from WATERDAMHOEK
and the French (18th Corps) were to advance
with their right just south of ZONNEBEKE-
WATERDAMHOEK road, thus giving the
Battalion a frontage of about 800 yards.
The line of country over which the Battn.
was to advance was, as far as the PASSCHEN-
DALE - BECELAERE main road which runs
along the top of a big (for Belgium) ridge
fairly steep up-hill, and fairly wooded.
From the above road eastwards the
ground slopes down gradually to the
HEULEBEEK stream. For the first 6 or
700 yards it is absolutely open cultivated
land, the only cover being a few scattered
farms and a line of houses running
along the top of the ridge on each side
of the road.
The part allotted to the Staffords was
however wooded most of the way.
About 700 yards east of the road there
are a number of small and medium
sized woods which afforded cover from
view but proved themselves absolute
shell traps - the whole of this piece of
country was covered with empty trenches
mostly hurriedly dug, some by the Germans

and some by the French. The latter had previously advanced across this ground but had been later compelled to retreat.

After 'A' Company had advanced and deployed it was seen that the frontage was so great that 'B' Company were sent up to fill the gap between A's left and the French: later 'C' and lastly (about 3 p.m.) 'D' Company were sent on in support with orders to work rather towards the left of our section of ground.

When 'B' Company had crossed the main road along the ridge the headquarters of the Battalion moved up into an old German so-called bombproof trench just west of the crest line near a battered school. There was an artillery observation post in this trench. While we were there the ridge was getting a terrific shelling [and one "black maria" came right into our trench within two yards of Willan completely burying his servant whom we however afterwards dug out quite uninjured]

During the advance eastwards from the ridge the battalion came under a terrific shell fire as well as rifle fire and 'A' Company especially lost very heavily.

Poor Prince Maurice was killed outright just on top

OCT | of the ridge and also Capt Wells (Buffs S.R) attached.
The following [4 Officers] were wounded - [Capt. Willis, Capt. Llewellyn (3rd Somersets attached) 2nd Lt. Hone and 2nd Lieut. Sweeting (Seriously).]
Total casualties for day - 24 killed, 130 wounded, and 19 missing.
As soon as it was nearly dark Willan and I went up to the firing line then about 800 yards east of the ridge and began to sort out the companies and arrange for improving the old and indifferent French trenches in which they nearly all were.

28th. The Battalion having improved their trenches remained in occupation of them all day under fairly heavy shell fire. Poor Teddy Waring was killed in his trench by a shell.
The Headquarters were in a cottage just behind a wood. Into which we had moved just before daylight from another house behind B and D companies trenches. Cpt Deeley and Rfn Wilcock were hit inside this house by bullets, the former being killed.

29th. On this day we were subjected to the heaviest shelling we had experienced so far during the war, being as we

Oct. were at the point of the Salient which our line formed we were naturally liable to shell fire from three directions. However the Battalion did not lose at all heavily as we feared it would.
One shell came in through the end wall of a sort of outhouse which joined on to our Headquarters house and the base of it came right through the wall of the room in which we were all sitting without doing more damage than throwing some of our food about! During the evening we spent several hours making a good dug-out on the edge of the wood for ourselves, and very glad we were of it next day.
Casualties for day were only 2 Rfn. wounded.

0th Another terrific day's shelling by far the heaviest we had had followed by an infantry attack which was directed mostly against the Staffords on our right. The part of it coming against our trenches was fairly easily beaten off, but 'D' (the left of our line) lost heavily. "A" Company had gone down during the night for a day's rest behind the ridge near the road

Oct. | but owing to the attack on the Battalion they were sent up to the ridge near the road where they had as bad a shelling as anyone, and anything but a rest. 2nd Lieut Casey was killed by a shell with this Company.

In the evening "A" Company were brought up again, two platoons (2nd Lieut Birkett and 2nd Lieut Collins) reinforcing "D" Company who had lost heavily, and 2 platoons remaining in support in some houses for the night and moving into the wood in front of our Hd Qrs. before daylight.

Total Casualties:- 1 Officer (2nd Lt Casey) Killed.
                   1 --- (2nd Lt Slater) wounded.
Other ranks:- 4 killed, 10 wounded.

31st Capt. Denison, Lt Gough, the Sgt. Major, Sgt O'Leary and a few others went down to poor Prince Maurice's funeral in YPRES.

    We had another attack preceded by another terrific bombardment. We sent our two reserve platoons ("A" Company) off to re-inforce the Stafford's who were very hard pressed at one time. During the day Capt Beauchamp Seymour was badly wounded in the head. Other casualties 10 h.e.t and Rft. wounded.

In the evening after dark about 10-30pm. our section of the line was taken over by some dismounted French cavalry and cyclists, the Staffords remaining in their positions.

6th Brigade.
2nd Division.

1st BATTALION

KING'S ROYAL RIFLE CORPS

NOVEMBER 1914

1st Battalion The King's Royal Rifle Corps.

November 1914

Nov. 1st. The Battalion arrived at the farm about 2 a.m. where they had been on the morning of the 27th Oct. and bivouacked round it for the night, the Officers sleeping in a barn. We remained there till about 10 a.m. when we were moved on to act as Divisional Reserve under Col. Westmacott at the N.W. corner of the POLYGONE Wood. Casualties 2 Rfn. wounded.

We were not left there long however, as about mid-day we were moved off with three Companies of the Berks to HOOGE Chateau to support the 1st Division. About 4 p.m. we were ordered to take over a section of the trenches running south from the HOOGE-GHELUVELT road. We took over from several different regiments including the S.W. Borderers, Gloucesters, &c. Capt. Willan was put in command of a section of the line consisting of 1st Coldstreams (200 men) ourselves and the Berks (3 Companies). Half of B Company (under Gough)

NOV.	were on the left about 100 yards S of the main road joining up with the 1st Coldstream Guards under Christie Miller. Then came 'D' and 'C' Companies the latter joining up with one Company of the Berks. Half of 'B' Company under 2nd Lieut. Richards were in support (i.e. behind 'C' Coy.) close behind the right centre of our line and the 2 Berks. Coys. (under Major Finch) were in support at the cross roads on the main road about 300 yards in rear of the trenches.
2nd.	Our Headquarters until daylight remained in some dug outs about 60 yards behind the firing line, but just before daylight they moved back into the wood near some dug outs occupied by our reserve Coy ('A').
	Our 2nd Battn. had occupied until our arrival the trenches taken over by the Berks and after handing over they moved back in the direction of HOOGE. After staying for a time in the dug-outs, Willan, Miller and I moved into the basement of the chateau in the wood. About 11am we received a message from Christie Miller who commanded the Coldstream Battalion on our left saying

that he believed that the other part of his line north of the road had broken as he was being enfiladed from his left flank. This message Capt. Dillon sent on to Major Finch (Berks) immediately asking him to help in any way he could. Major Finch sent back a message to say he was sending up two platoons at once to help on the north side of the main road. Capt Dillon then went out on to the main road himself and up towards the crossroads where he saw the Berks lying across the road and the Germans facing them. "A" Company (reserve) was then sent up also along the north side of the road to re-inforce the Berks and an orderly was sent back towards HOOGE and 1st Division for further help. The 2nd Bn. K.R.R. were sent up by them to help on both sides of the main road and they were followed up by several other weak battalions – Welsh Regiment, South Wales Borderers, Loyal N. Lancs and Gloucesters and the gap in the line was thus filled, the line being withdrawn about 300 yards until it was approximately along the eastern edge of the wood. The Germans however

Nov.	still occupied the trenches taken from the Coldstreams. The pressure on the north side of the road had also been relieved very considerably by the fact that the French happened to be making an advance on GHELUVELT from the North and their right reached the neighbourhood of VELLDHOEK just at the critical moment. We (Battn. Headquarters) were quite in ignorance of what had happened to our own three Companies 'B', 'C' and 'D' who were in the trenches on the right of the Coldstreams as our Headquarters were with the reserve Company "A" back in the wood from the front edge of which even it was impossible to see the trenches owing to the latter being down on a forward slope. Casualties - 'A' Coy. 3 Rfn. Killed. 9 wounded (including 2nd Lt. Collins) Other Coys - 9 Officers, 437 other ranks missing.
3rd	Battn. H.Qrs. and 'A' Company in close support to Berks in woods west of GHELUVELT. Heavy shelling all day but hardly any casualties. Turned out 3 times during night on account of heavy firing. Casualties - 2 Rfn. wounded.

NOV.
4th Same position. Tremendous shelling all day and two German attacks one in morning and one in evening. Major Warre DSO came from 2nd Battalion and assumed command. Heavy rain during evening and night. Casualties - 2 Rfn. wounded.

5th Several German attacks during day accompanied by heavy shelling. Rifleman Onslow killed in mess dug out and L/Cpl. Edwards and one other Rifleman wounded. 6p.m. Battalion marched to N.W. corner of POLYGONE wood and reported to Col. Westmacott commanding 5th Brigade.
Not called out during night.
Given dinner by Coldstream mess
Transport Officers' house blown in in morning just after we had moved off.

6th Improved dug outs after breakfast but ordered re-join 6th Brigade S. of ZONNEBEKE before mist lifted.
Marched at 9 a.m. went into dug outs near 6th Bde. H.Q. and improved them
At 6p.m. Denison and 'A' Company (Battalion) moved out to take up second line in rear of Connaughts in case of alarm. Moved back at 10pm and made fresh dug outs further up hill our old ones being required for Berks. H.Q. moved to cottage close to Brigade H. Qrs.   Quiet night.

NOV.
7th. 5a.m. Headquarters made dug outs close
to where 'A' Company's were made the
previous night.
7.15 a.m. Headquarters and 'A' Company
moved up to H.L.I. headquarters as we
were told one of their trenches had been
partially occupied by the enemy.
Casualties - 1 Pte. R.A.M.C. attached wounded.
'A' Company were ordered to clear this
trench but a counter order came from the
Brigade before this could be carried out,
but 'A' Company remained under orders
of Col. Wolfe Murray (commanding H.L.I.)
At 4 p.m. a portion of the Connaughts' line
gave way under shell fire and all
available men were sent forward immediately
in case the Germans advanced.
'A' Company was taken from the H.L.I. and
with the Berkshires were ordered to clear
the Germans out of the trenches. A fresh
line of out posts was however made by
7.30 p.m. and no further action taken
against the enemy.
'A' Company occupied a 2nd line in rear
of Connaughts for the night.
8th. 'A' Company about 7.30 a.m. took over
4 "Points d'appui" in rear of Connaughts
line with one platoon close behind

NOV. Connaught's trenches, the latter was withdrawn to Battⁿ Headquarters at 4 p.m. Casualties - 1 R⁺⁻ wounded.

9th. Easy morning. Changed our Headquarters about 300 yards to another house where our dressing station had been on 27th. Oct. A certain amount of shelling.
'A' Company under Willan took over H.L.I. trench.

10th. Capt. Denison sent down sick.
Court of Inquiry, at which I gave evidence in evening, re missing Containers.
'A' Company still in H.L.I. trench.

11th. Woke up at 5.30 a.m. by a shrapnel hitting our roof. No other shells particularly near us all day, but French battery and ZONNEBEKE ridge shelled pretty heavily all day. Very heavy rain began about 5 p.m. but stopped about 8 p.m.
'A' Company still holding H.L.I. trench.
Heard of sinking of "Emden".

12th. About 6.30 a.m. I looked out of the window of our Headquarter House and saw about 50 Germans, 1,200 yards away, in front of and among some houses near the cross roads N. of 6th Kilometer on the BECELAERE road. Apparently they had broken through the French line, near that point

Nov. and taken up a position just west of the road. Sgt O'Leary, the Servants and Headquarter signallers manned the windows and some holes in the roof and opened fire. We told the Artillery officer who was in charge of two 18 pr. Field guns about 50 yards from our house, he turned his guns round and after he had fired a few shells the Germans got up in a body and ran out of sight from us behind the houses: our guns continued to fire on the houses but the Germans continued to hold the cross roads and the French failed to dis-lodge them.
We kept the Headquarters with their equipment on all day and some of the H.L.I. and 1st Coldstreams were sent up in the afternoon to fill the gap in the line.
'A' Company still holding trenches had two Riflemen killed

13th. A fairly quiet night.
About 7 a.m. in the morning we heard that the Germans had broken through one Company of the H.L.I. near the School house on the ridge. The ridge had been very heavily shelled all the morning. The reserve companies were sent from Brigade reserve and the line re-established

NOV. during the day but the Staffords in the wood east of the BECELAERE road were withdrawn during the night and the line put along the eastern side of the road.
In the evening and during most of the day it rained heavily, and as Capt. Willan had a bad cold and had had his eyes filled with mud by a bullet in the trenches I went up to relieve him there about 9 p.m. I went to sleep in a dug out and suddenly woke up to find I couldn't move as the side had fallen in and covered me with earth. I was however soon dug out.
Capt. Tate joined with a draft of 170 R.fn.

14th A day of very heavy showers. We had a certain amount of shelling but only one man wounded by shell fire.
The enemy's snipers were very active and as our trenches formed a right angle they were very liable to be enfiladed both by rifle and shell fire
Our casualties for the day were 5 killed (all shot in the head by snipers) and 3 wounded.

15th One of the most unpleasant days I have ever spent. Rain and a little snow in the morning. Our hut leaking continuously, and the trenches a sea of mud

NOV. 29

and water, in addition to which the Germans, (having apparently) spotted some new loop holes I had had made during the night, gave us a really nasty shelling with "Fluffies" (big howitzer shells). These completely enfiladed the part of our trenches in which our Headquarters were. Two burst right inside our trenches one right above and only a few feet from the top of our H.Qrs dug out in which 6 of us, 2nd Lt Birkett C/S.M. Tedder, 3 others and myself were. Six pieces of shell came through the wooden roof, one piece hitting the bank within a foot of my head, another going through Birkett's burberry, and another piece through a book someone was reading, but none was touched — great luck.

The above two shells killed 2 and wounded 9 men in the trench near our dugout. We were feeling rather depressed but were much cheered by a message passed down by the Worcesters that we were to be relieved by the French in the evening. Soon after dark a party of about 30 Germans crawled up to the wire about 20 yards in front of the left of our trenches; we opened fire and by the time I could

NOV.	
	fire a shot from a VERYS pistol they had gone. About 11.30p.m. 150 men of the IX French Corps arrived to relieve us. The relief passed off all right, the Germans sniped at us all the time but we did not have a man hit which was lucky as we had to move along the top of the trenches behind the French to get out.
16th	The Brigade marched to a wood on the railway near HOOGE Chateau where we arrived about 6 a.m. It was pouring with rain and the wood was an absolute swamp. On arrival at the wood we found Major G.C. Shakerley, D.S.O. had arrived with a draft of 88 R.fn.
	The Battalion remained there until 8-45 p.m. when they marched to billets at N.W. corner of YPRES arriving there about 11 p.m.
17th	1 p.m. I was sent to arrange billets for Battalion at WESTOUTRE as the latter was marching there at 4 p.m. I arranged billets and at 10 p.m. received orders to return to YPRES as the move had been ~~ordered~~ altered to 4 a.m. (on 18th). I did not get back to Battalion Headquarters till
18th	nearly 1 a.m. as my horse had a shoe loose.
	At 4 a.m. I started with brigade and then

NOV.
rode on, picked up billeting party at WESTOUTRE and rode on to arrange billets at CASTRE. A wonderful view at top of the hill near MONT-DES-CATS.
Battalion arrived at CASTRE and went into billets about 2 p.m.

Casualties. 23rd Aug. 18th Nov. 1914.
Officers.

Killed	Wounded	Missing	Accidently shot
5	23	9	1

also 1 Offr. R.A.M.C. attached died of wounds.
(Capt. H.S. Ranken).

- Other ranks -

Killed	Wounded	Missing	Accidently shot
90*	417	490	2

* Exclusive of died of wounds which are shown as wounded if still living when admitted to field ambulance or Hospital.

Total casualties all ranks exclusive of admissions to hospital sick – 1037.

Capt. E. A. Bradford accidently shot in foot.

Casualties - Officers. 23rd Aug. - 18th Nov. 48/32

1.	1st Sept.	Lt. P.G. Chaworth-Musters	Wounded
2.	10th "	Lt. & Adjt. R.H. Woods	"
3.	"	Lt. A.L. Bonham Carter	"
4.	"	2/Lt. H.W. Butler	"
5.	"	2/Lt. R.A. Banon	" remained at duty.
6.	14th "	Capt. A.F.C. Maclachlan D.S.O.	"
7.	"	Capt. G. Makins, M.V.O.	"
8.	"	2/Lt. H.C. Lloyd	"
9.	19th	Lt. J.S. Alston	"
10.	20th	Lt. F.W. Cavendish Bentinck	"
11.	27th	Lt. Col. E. Northey	"
12.	28th	Lt. A.M. Brocklehurst	"
13.	8th Oct.	Lt. C.G.E. Clowes	"
14.	14th	Lt. & Q.M. A. Harman	"
15.	26th	2/Lt. W.G. Cronk (3rd Buffs. att'd.)	Killed
16.	"	Lt. E.G.W. Bourke	Wounded
17.	"	2/Lt. K.H.W. Ward	"
18.	27th	Lt. H.H. Prince Maurice of Battenburg K.C.V.O.	Killed
19.	"	Capt. W. Wells (3rd Buffs)	"
20.	"	Capt. A.L.Y. Willis, 5 K.R.R.	Wounded
21.	"	Capt. W.W. Llewellyn (3 Somersets)	"
22.	"	2/Lt. T.N. Howe	"
23.	"	2/Lt. H. Sweeting, 5 K.R.R.	"
24.	28th	2/Lt. E.R. Warring	Killed
25.	30th	2/Lt. J. Casey	"
26.	"	2/Lt. R.M. Slater	Wounded
27.	31st	Capt. B. Seymour	"

Continued.

28.	2nd Nov.	2Lt C. Collins	wounded
29	"	Capt. W.P. Lynes. 5KRR.	missing
30	"	Capt. H.E. Ward. 3rd Buffs	"
31	"	Lt. Ara Wakefield Saunders.	"
32	"	Lt. G.V.H. Gough.	"
33	"	Lt. C.H. Reynard.	"
34	"	Lt. C.F. Schoon.	"
35	"	Lt. R. Richards.	"
36	"	Lt. S. Lucas	"
37	"	Lt. S. Wadner.	"

1914
Nov.

18th. Battalion in rest Billets at CAESTRE.

23rd Capt. L.G. Grazebrook. Joined.
" E.P. Shakerley. "

29th Col. E. Northey. re-joined from wounded.

30th A draft of 365 N.C.O.s and Rfn. joined
The following Officers also joined:-
Capt. F.C. Norbury, Lt. W.W.W. Godman.
Lt. W.A. Grenville Grey, Lt. A.R. Herron
Lt. D. Henderson, Lt. S.J. Steadman.
Lt. D.G. Wigan.

Court of Inquiry
Reference events.

2nd November 1914

War Office Reference.
121/France/5568

K.R.R.C.

6th Brigade
2nd Division.

1st BATTALION

KING'S ROYAL RIFLE CORPS

DECEMBER 1914:

1st Battalion The King's Royal Rifle Corps.

December 1914

DEC.

4th A draft of 143 N.C.Os and Rfn. joined.

10th Capt. T. F. Tate exchanged with Capt. A. L. Bonham Carter from 2nd Battn.

12th Lieuts E. A. Pauly and A. E. Messer joined.

15th Lieut. H. Else joined on promotion from R. Bde.

17th Lieut and Q.Mr A. Harman re-joined from wounded.

Bn. continues in rest Billets.

1914.
22nd
Dec:

8.45 a.m. the Brigade left CAESTRE, in Motor Buses and went via HAZEBROUCK - ST. VENANT and LILLERS to BETHUNE, where we got out of the buses about 12 NOON. The Battalion used 33 buses in all.
About 1 pm. Battn. marched from BETHUNE to BEUVRY where they halted for about an hour.
At about 3 p.m. Battn. continued its march towards CUINCHY and after dark took over trenches from the Connaught Rangers (Lt. Col. Ravenshaw).
The line of these ran from the BETHUNE - LA BASSEE road to the LA BASSEE Canal both inclusive. Three Companies were in the firing line (B. C & D) and one in reserve (A). 'B' Coy. connected with the French having one platoon south of the BETHUNE - LA BASSEE road, then came 'C' in the centre and then 'D' with their left on the Canal.
The Battalion Headquarters were in CUINCHY in a large house.
We had an amusing incident during the night: at about 2am Col. Northey, the Medical Officer and myself were asleep in a room in the basement when we heard a couple of shots which sounded

Dec: 2

as if they had been fired from very close range hit the wall. Presently we heard someone just outside talking very bad French we therefore put out our light and had just done so when someone outside pulled away the boards and rags which we had in our window to keep our light from showing, put the muzzle of his rifle in through our window and loosed off. The Colonel and I got outside as quickly as we could (the doctor was immobile having taken his boots off) and went and fetched our guard which was about 200 yards away down a communication trench: we then surrounded the house and captured our enemies who however proved to be only a patrol of about Six of the Berkshire Regt. who had seen our light and taken us for Germans. (as we had them). It was lucky for the man at our window that we had all left our revolvers upstairs or he would have certainly been shot. Casualties - One Rfn (M.G. Section) wounded during the relief and one other Rfn wounded.

23rd Colonel Northey and I went round all our trenches which took us 4 hours, the going being very deep in places and some of the communication

Dec:

trenches being very narrow: we also went to see the Headquarters of the South Staffords on the northern side of the Canal - crossing by the lock near our Headquarters.
It snowed from about 9 to 11 a.m.
There was pretty heavy sniping going on all day on both sides and the Germans were bombarding 'D' and 'C' Coys. trenches with trench mortars.
The casualties for the day were :-
    1 Rfn. Killed, 4 wounded.

24th. Quiet day except for usual sniping.
Casualties - 3 Rfn Killed (Sgt. Smith, Cpl. Woolgar). 2 ... Wounded.

25th. Xmas Day. Hard frost and everything quiet.
Battalion was relieved by 1st Kings Regt. in trenches and moved back into Brigade Reserve on LA BASSEE - BETHUNE road.
The 1st Company of the Kings Regt arrived about 1-30 pm and our last Company (A) to be relieved did not get into billets till 7 pm.
Casualties - 7 wounded.

26th. At 2 pm the Battalion handed over its billets to Loyal North Lancs. Regt. (2nd Bde. relieved 6th Bde.) and marched via BEUVRY - LEQUESNOY - PONT TOURNANT

Dec:
to LE HAMEL and went into billets there about 5 p.m.

27th. The 6th Brigade remained in billets at ESSARS and LE HAMEL as Corps Reserve. Heavy rain nearly all day.
Lt. Col Davidson (S. Staffs.) assumed temporary command of the Brigade, General Fanshawe having taken temporary command of 2nd Division.

28th. The Battalion remained in billets in LE HAMEL.
There was a tremendous storm during the evening and night but not much rain.

29th. The 6th Brigade moved into billets near LOCON in 1st Corps reserve.
Battalion left LE HAMEL at 1-30 p.m. and marched to billets near LES LOBES (about 1 mile north of LOCON) arriving about 3.15 p.m. Fine afternoon.

30th. Brigade remained in 1st Corps reserve.
Battalion remained in billets about LES LOBES.

31st. Brigade received orders to relieve 4th (Guards) Brigade in trenches on 2nd January.

2nd Division

War Diaries

1st Battn. Kings Royal Rifles

January to June 1915

6th Infantry Brigade.
2nd Division.

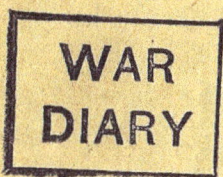

1st BATTN. THE KING'S ROYAL RIFLE CORPS.

JANUARY

1 9 1 5

1st Battn. The King's Royal Rifle Corps.

January 1915.

1915.
Jan 1st. The Battalion received orders at 8.30 a.m.

JAN. to be ready to move at very short notice, but remained in billets at LES LOBES.

2nd. Battalion left LES LOBES at 2.45 p.m. and took over trenches from 1st Herts Regt. (T) and Irish Guards, as 6th Bde. relieved 4th (Guards) Brigade.

"A" and "B" Coys. were in front line, "D" in support and "C" in reserve.

"A" Coy., on whose left was our Machine Gun section covering a gap of about 500 yards, to the Oxfords, took over from the Herts and B Coy. from half of the Irish Guards: the other half of the latter was relieved by the Kings Regt. who consequently connected with our right.

The Battalion Headquarters were in a farm house on the RUE DU BOIS about 500 yards West of the village of RICHEBOURG L'AVOUE and our line of trenches ran approximately 200 yards east of the RICHEBOURG L'AVOUE – FESUIBERT road on which our right, being thrown back, rested.

The trenches were very wet most of the communication trenches being too flooded to use.

The relief passed off quietly.

JAN.   8

The German trenches on our right were about 100 yds in front of 'A' Coys' right, while from the left of 'B' Coy' [Company] they were about 450 yards away.

3rd. Quiet day in trenches, rain most of the day.
At dark "A" and "B" Coys. were relieved in the trenches by 'C' and 'D' respectively.
About 1 p.m. the Germans shelled a house next to the one occupied by our reserve machine gunners and put two shells near our Headquarters but did no harm.
There was a little sniping all day.
Casualties for the day were :- 1 Rfn. wounded.

4th. Another quiet day. Certain amount of sniping and our trenches were shelled by enemy's trench mortar.
'C' and 'D' Coys were relieved at dark by 'A' and 'B' Coys: an extraordinarily dark night which made the relief very difficult.
During the night a man of the 16th Westphalian Regiment (lately drafted from the Ersatz) walked into 'B' Coy. trench and was taken prisoner.
Casualties for day:-
5 wounded (1 accidentally).

JAN.

5th. Quiet day. 'A' Coy. was bombed during morning by trench mortar.
'A' and 'B' Coys. were relieved at dark by 'C' and 'D' the relief being carried out much more quickly than before.
Casualties for day:-
1 L/Cpl died of wounds, 1 Rfn. killed, 1 Cpl and 7 Rfn. wounded.
Lieut Musters and one platoon of 'C' Coy. started new trench towards 5th Bde.

6th. Fine day and some sun in the morning. Level of water in trenches consequently fell a bit.
Germans started throwing trench mortar bombs at 'C' Coy. during morning but stopped as soon as our howitzers (60th Battery) opened on their trenches.
'A' and 'B' Coys. relieved 'C' and 'D' at dark and work on new trench towards 5th Bde. was continued by Lt. Birkett's platoon.
About 10 pm. heavy rain began.
Casualties for day:-
1 Rfn. killed. 3 Wounded.
2nd Lieut Maclachlan who had gone out to visit an advanced post of 'B' Coy. in an old disused trench was wounded in the foot.

JAN.
7th. The rain which had begun the previous night continued steadily all day, and the level of the water in trenches of course rose again.

'B' Coy's new fire trench which had been quite dry, by 6pm had a foot of water in it.

Very quiet day.

At dark 'A' and 'B' Coys. were relieved by 'C' and 'D'. 2nd Lieut Slater's platoon continuing the trench towards 5th Bde. Casualties: 2 wounded.

8th. Good deal of rain at intervals all day and very strong wind.

About 3.45 pm one of our Lyddite shells unfortunately dropped into 'C' Coys. trenches killing Captain F.C. Norbury and wounding badly Lieut. P.G. Chaworth-Musters and 2nd Lieut. B.F. Whiteley who were together in one part of the trench.

At dark 'C' and 'D' Coys. were relieved by 'A' and 'B'.

Major Armytage and Capt. Denison rejoined and assumed command of 'C' and 'D' Coys. respectively.

Besides the Officers we had one L/Cpl killed on an advanced post and two Rfn. wounded one of whom died in Hospital

13

JAN.
9th. Quiet day except for our artillery, which was active at times.
The Germans put a few Howitzer shells near our reserve Coys. billets but did no harm.
At dark C and D Coys. relieved A and B.
A certain amount of rain during day.
Casualties - nil.

10th. In order to divert the attention of the enemy from a small attack made by the 2nd Bde. on the left of our old trenches near CUINCHY a heavy artillery bombardment began by all our guns at 1.45 p.m.: our Coys. in the trenches fired short bursts of rapid fire and our trench mortars also fired apparently with good results.
As it was a bright sunny afternoon it was easy to observe our artillery fire which apparently was very accurate and to which the Germans only made a feeble reply.
They were observed running about from one part of their trenches to another presumably into dug outs further back, and one or two who tried to climb up into a loft of a ruined house

JAN. 14

opposite our trenches were shot by our snipers.
At dark 'A' and 'B' Coys. relieved 'C' and 'D'.
After dark rain started again.
Casualties - 2 Killed, 1 wounded who afterwards died.

11th. A fine day except for a few heavy showers.
We had another piece of bad luck about 1.45 pm. a heavy shell fell into our right trench killing 2nd Lieut. D. Henderson and one Rifleman and wounding 2 others.
At dark 'A' and 'B' Coys. were relieved by 'C' and 'D'.
About 6 pm. rain started again.
Casualties: 1 Rfn. (died of wounds) 3 Rfn. Wounded.

12th. A very quiet day both as regards shelling and sniping.
We were very sorry to hear during the morning that Lt. Chaworth Musters had died of his wounds in BETHUNE.
The weather kept fine and the level of the water fell a little.
At dark "A" and 'B' Coys. relieved 'C' and 'D' in the trenches.
2nd Lieut. R. Fellowes joined and was posted to 'C' Coy.
Casualties - 1 Rfn. Killed. 1 Wounded.

JAN
13th. Wet and very quiet day.
'C' and 'D' Coys. relieved 'A' and 'B' in the trenches at dark.
During the day the Germans fired a few 77 m.m. shells at the billets of the front line Coys. but there were absolutely no casualties for the day.

14th. Another quiet day.
During the morning one Rifleman was shot dead in billets.
No rain all day.
About 3 p.m. a German convoy of a dozen wagons was observed arriving and "parking" under cover of a farm about 2.500 yards in front of our left Company. The convoy was shelled by the 60th Battery with lyddite, apparently with good effect.
At dark 'A' and 'B' Coys. relieved 'C' and 'D' in the trenches.
Casualties for day - 1 Rfn. wounded.

15th. Quiet day.
The Battalion was relieved in the trenches by the 1st Herts (T): the 4th Bde. taking over from the 6th.
The reserve and supporting Coys. moved off about 2.30 p.m. and reached their billets in HINGES about 5.30 p.m.

JA.   17

'A' and 'B' Coys. who had been in the trenches did not get in until 11 p.m. as their relief could not be carried out till after dark owing to the water in the communication trenches.
Casualties for day - 1 Rfn. Killed.

16th. Brigade remained in billets near HINGES and LOCON in divisional reserve.
2nd Lieut G. A. Fisher joined the Battalion.

17th. Brigade in Divisional Reserve. [Battalion remained in billets at HINGES]
Some snow in afternoon.

18th. Fairly heavy snow in morning; but this turned to rain in the evening.

19th. All snow nearly gone. Went out shooting in afternoon with Bonham Carter and Pardoe's 16 bore gun. Got two partridges and a hare: Brooke and two others (South Irish Horse) and some Signallers and stretcher bearers beat for us.

20th. The 6th Brigade relieved the 4th Brigade in the trenches. Battalion forming part of Brigade Reserve, moved into new billets at MESPLAUX (1 mile E. of LOCON).
Very scattered billets, 'A' Coy only being in farm with Headquarters.

21st. Battalion remained in billets at MESPLAUX. Fine frosty morning.

22nd. - Ditto -

JAN.
23rd. The Battalion took over its old trenches near RICHEBOURG L'AVOUE from the Staffords. 'C' and 'D' Coys. took over the trenches. 'A' and 'B' Coys. being in reserve.
The 39th Garhwal Rifles connected with our left Coy. ('D') but there was a gap of 3 or 400 yards between their right and our left which was patrolled by night.
'C' and 'D' Coys. began taking over at 5.30 p.m. and the relief was complete by 7 p.m.
During the night 'D' Coy. assisted by East Anglian R.E. (T) constructed a breastwork in the centre of the above mentioned gap, and 'C' Coy. a similar one in the gap on their right left there owing to the wet state of the ground.

24th. A quiet day: fine but cloudy.
There was not much sniping but we were unlucky and had 2nd Lieut. W. W. Godman killed by a sniper in the right part of 'D' Coys trenches close to the point of the Salient which our line formed. We also had 4 Rfn. killed and 1 wounded.

25th. About 7.30 a.m the German Artillery began to shell the houses occupied by our supports, and the house where our left hand machine gun was: While Lieut. Wigan the Machine Gun Officer was

JAN 1

turning the men out of the house to take cover behind a bank he was knocked down by a shell but not hurt beyond receiving a bad shock.]

About 8 a.m. very heavy rifle fire began some distance to our left: this proved to be an attack on the 8th Division between whom and our left were two ~~Inf~~ Indian Brigades. After about an hour the firing died down but there were bursts of fire from that direction at intervals during the day. As soon as the firing was first heard the two reserve Coys. 'A' and 'B' stood to arms and the small supporting works near our Headquarters were occupied in case of an attack.

There was however no infantry attack on our front or on that of the Brigades on our right or left. [we however heard that the Germans had taken some of the 1st Division trenches near GIVENCHY but these had later been retaken by our local counter attacks, and that the Germans had broken through on the BETHUNE - LA BASSEE road.]

Casualties for day - 2 killed. 3 wounded.

JAN'
26th. A quiet day and no rain.
During the morning, 2nd Lieut. Austin, R.F.A. was killed by a sniper on the road between the Headquarters of the Companies in the trenches and the house occupied by the machine gun "Class" on our left: we had been warned when we first took over from the Herts that this road was dangerous but we had never had anyone hit walking along it, although it had been used fairly regularly by day as well as by night.
At dark 'C' and 'D' Coys. were relieved in the trenches by 'A' and 'B'.
A report had been received that the German trenches in the neighbourhood of "The Orchard" opposite our right Coy. were seen from the 'Brewery' to be much more strongly held than usual, also a gap had been noticed in the German wire opposite this point: this, coupled with the fact that German re-inforcements were reported to have arrived on the western front and that the next day was the Kaiser's birthday made us very much on the look out for an attack during the night.
Casualties - 2 Rfn. wounded.

JAN.
27th. The Battalion stood to arms at 5 a.m. but the day turned out to be one of the quietest we had had for some time.
There was hardly any shelling and very little sniping.
A fine day.   Casualties - NIL.

28th. Another quiet day: a sharp frost.
In the afternoon the Battalion was relieved in the trenches by the 2nd South Staffords
The reserve Coys. ('C' and 'D') were relieved about 4 p.m. and the Coys. in the trenches ('A' and 'B') began to be relieved about 6 p.m. and the whole battalion marched to its old billets in MESPLAUX as Divisional Reserve.
Casualties for day - 1 Rfn. wounded.

29th. A sharp black frost during the night and morning.
About 9 a.m. heavy artillery and rifle fire was audible from the direction of CUINCHY, and about 9-40 a.m. orders were received from 2nd Division that Battalion was to "Stand by" ready to move if required.
About 1 p.m. the order to "Stand by" was cancelled: we afterwards heard that during the morning the Germans had made another heavy attack on the South side of the LA. BASSÉE Canal

JAN.

near CUINCHY but had been repulsed with heavy loss, by 1st Division.

30th. The Battalion remained in billets at MESPLAUX in Divisional Reserve.
During the morning a thaw set in and by the evening the ground was everywhere quite soft again although the ice in the ditches had not melted. A fine day and quite warm.
Two additional Machine Guns were received by the Battalion.

31st. The Battalion remained in billets at MESPLAUX in Divisional Reserve.
1/16° During the morning there was a strong south wind and some snow but it afterwards turned to slight rain in the afternoon.

6th Infantry Brigade.
2nd Division.

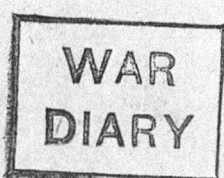

1st BATTN. THE KING'S ROYAL RIFLE CORPS.

F E B R U A R Y

1 9 1 5

Attached:

Reconnaissance Report
of 27.2.15 & Map.

1st Battn. The King's Royal Rifle Corps.

February 1915.

FEBY.
1st. 6th Inf. Brigade was relieved by Bareilley Brigade.
Battalion left MESPLAUX and marched to its old billets in HINGES starting at 1.30 p.m. and arriving about 3.30 p.m. A rather dull day but quite warm and no rain.
2nd Lieut A. Hoare and 2nd Lieut G. Hayhurst France joined the Battalion with a draft of 29 N.C.O's and Men.

FEBY.
26

2nd | Battalion remained in billets at HINGES. Rain most of the morning. C.O. and O.C. 'C' and 'D' Coys. rode to GIVENCHY to reconnoitre new line near there to be taken over by Battn. next day.

3rd | 6th Brigade relieved 3rd Brigade in trenches about GIVENCHY.
Battalion left HINGES at 12-30 p.m. and marched via AVELETTE - BETHUNE - and along Southern tow-path of LA. BASSÉE Canal.
'C' and 'D' Coys. crossed the Canal at PONT FIXE and went direct to take over trenches from South Wales Borderers and 4th Royal Welsh Fusiliers (T) in and West of GIVENCHY arriving about 4.15 p.m.
Battn. Headquarters and 2 Reserve Companies ('A' and 'B') crossed Canal by pontoon bridge about 1000 yards West of PONT FIXE and went into billets about "WINDY CORNER" (about 900 yards. W.S.W. of GIVENCHY).
"C" Coy. on right took over what was known as "SCOTTISH TRENCH" and connected with the King's on their right.
'D' Coy. were on the left of 'C' and echeloned back behind the latter facing nearly north, the right of 'D' being in fact straight behind the left of SCOTTISH TRENCH.
On 'D's left there was a considerable

FEB<u>Y</u>.   28

gap between them and the right of the
5<u>th</u> Brigade but the ground in this neighbourhood was too boggy to be passable except
after frost.
 'C' Coy. had 3 platoons in the trenches and
1 in support - in front of their right was
the WHITE HOUSE which was about 80 yards
from our trenches and was patrolled at
night by both Germans and ourselves.
During the night L'Cpl. Foley ('C' Coy.) was
wounded by German Snipers in this house
while in charge of a patrol sent to visit
it. His patrol had been there earlier
in the night and found it unoccupied
but on returning later the patrol was
fired on.
 Total casualties for day - 3 wounded.

4<u>th</u>. A fairly quiet day, fine and sunny.
There was a certain amount of shelling all
day. The Germans dropped about a dozen
8" howitzer shells near GIVENCHY CHURCH,
one of these unfortunately killed Sgt. Smith
(who had only arrived with the draft on
1<u>st</u> Feb<u>y</u>.) also a Rifleman, and badly
wounded two others, these casualties occurred
to a party who were apparently getting water
from a pump: the shells were dated 1896
and nearly half of them did not burst

FEB?

at all - the one that did the damage was filled with a yellow explosive which seemed not to detonate properly.
Total Casualties - 2 Killed
8 Wounded.

5th Another beautiful sunny day.
Rather less shelling than the day before.
During the afternoon 'A' and 'B' Coys. took over from 'C' and 'D'. ['A' relieving 'C' and 'B' - 'D'.]
Casualties for day - NIL.

6th. A fine day but not so much sun.
An attack was made on the brickfield east of CUINCHY by the 4th (Guards) Brigade, it was preceded by a very heavy artillery bombardment of which I got a good view from the roof of our H.Qrs house.
The attack began at 2.15p.m. after 15 minutes bombardment and we heard shortly afterwards that it had been a complete success and had resulted in the capture of 20 prisoners.
During the afternoon Sgt. French ('A' Coy) was killed by a bullet in Scottish Trench.
Soon after dark it began to rain.
Casualties for day - Sgt French killed only.

7th A fine day after wet night.
All morning Germans were very quiet but at 4 p.m. they began a heavy bombardment

FEB.

of the brickfield east of CUINCHY which the Guards had taken the previous day. We heard later that they had attempted to attack but our artillery which opened a heavy fire as soon as the German guns began to shell the brickfield, put a stop to it.

During the afternoon 'A' and 'B' Coys. were relieved in the trenches by 'C' and 'D' respectively, it was during the relief that the German bombardment began. About 6 p.m. 2nd Lieut G.V. Hordern joined with a draft of 75 N.C.O's and Riflemen. Casualties for day - 1 Rfn. died of wounds 3 wounded (including Sgt. Lodge).

8th. A fine sunny morning. The Germans spotted the draft which had arrived the previous night being marched past "WINDY CORNER" to be seen by the C.O. about 10 a.m. and consequently shelled our headquarters with shrapnel but did no damage.

Lieut. F.V. Crawhall joined the Battalion and was posted to 'A' Coy.

Casualties - 2 Killed. 2 Wounded.

9th. Windy morning; it began to rain about 11.30 a.m. and did not stop till about 5.30 pm.

FEB.Y

A very quiet day as regards shelling.
During the afternoon 'C' and 'D' Coys. were
relieved in the trenches by 'A' and 'B'.
Casualties - NIL.

10th Another very quiet day.
Casualties - NIL.

11th Quiet day.
In the afternoon 'A' and 'B' Coys. were relieved
in the trenches by 'C' and 'D'.
Casualties - 2 Rfn. Wounded

12th Cold morning. It was inclined to snow
about 8 a.m. but very little fell.
During the morning the Germans were rather
more active as regards shelling and put
a few shells near our Battn. H.Qrs. also
one over 'D' Coys. trenches which slightly
wounded two men, one of whom however
was not admitted to hospital.
One Rifleman of 'C' Coy. was also badly
wounded in the head by a sniper.
In the evening a post of one N.C.O. and 6
Riflemen was established at the WHITE
HOUSE opposite SCOTTISH TRENCH.
Casualties - 2 Rfn. wounded (one died on 14th).

13th Very wet and cold morning.
Quiet day.
In the afternoon 'C' and 'D' Coys. were relieved
in the trenches by 'A' and 'B'.

FEB^Y.

During the night the mine towards the WHITE HOUSE which had been started under the parapet of SCOTTISH TRENCH and broken through to the surface during the day, was continued to within about 5 yards of the sunk road by digging on the surface.

One L/Cpl. of 'A' Coy. with this digging party was wounded and died next day, also one Rifleman wounded.

14th. About 10 a.m. the French on the right of the 4th Brigade near the BETHUNE - LA BASSÉE road made an attack and in conjunction with the right of the 4th Brigade succeeded in taking a German trench thus straightening out the line.

In the evening heavy rain began and continued most of the night.

Captain C.A. Grazebrook admitted to Hospital sick.

One Rifleman wounded.

15th. Quiet day, hardly any shelling or sniping. Cold morning but fine sunny afternoon. In the afternoon 'C' and 'D' Coys. relieved 'A' and 'B' in the trenches.

During the relief of the King's on our right by the Berks. the Germans who had apparently noticed movement on the WINDY CORNER - GIVENCHY road shelled GIVENCHY village.

FEB.Y

The Berks. had two Officers wounded by these shells and also Lieut. Caldwell, R.F.A. was hit by one near the Keep.
Casualties for day - one Rifleman wounded.

16th. Fine sunny day.
The Germans were very quiet. Our aeroplanes were very active all day, and the Germans wasted a lot of shells on them.
During the morning we had two Lance Corporals of "C" Coy. killed while crawling about near the WHITE HOUSE searching dead Germans, also the L/Cpl. in charge of the WHITE HOUSE post was wounded.
We had one Rifleman killed by a Sniper while working in the main communication trench.
Total casualties for day - 3 killed, 3 wounded.

17th. Cold wind and rain all day.
During the morning a mountain gun was brought up just behind our trenches at FRENCH FARM and "registered" on the German trenches and breastworks opposite the 5th Brigade: the shooting appeared very good and the Germans were completely enfiladed and even taken in reverse by this fire. Absolutely no movement was however visible in these trenches which appear to be very lightly held.

FEBY

In the afternoon 'C' and 'D' Coys. were relieved in the trenches by 'A' and 'B'.
Casualties - NIL.

18th. Fine but windy day.
The artillery on both sides were pretty active all the morning and in the afternoon the Germans put a few shells very close to our Headquarters but did no harm.
On going round the trenches the amount of work done by the battalion since 3rd February is very noticeable: when we took over hardly any of the parapets were even bullet proof. We have remedied this, made numerous new traverses, also a "parados" in many places - most of the communication trenches and some of the fire trenches have now brick floors: we also have made two new communication trenches from WINDY CORNER to the ROAD RESERVE HOUSE which was occupied by the reserve platoon of the left Company. The Brigadier (General Fanshawe) on going round the Battalions' trenches on 17th. was much struck by the amount of work done and complimented the battalion on the great improvements effected in the trenches.
At 6.45 pm 2nd Lieut Else and Cpl. Hilton of 'A' Coy. worked their way up an old trench

FEBY.

or line of dugouts inside the orchard east of SCOTTISH TRENCH. They then threw 4 German hand bombs into the German main trench where it touched the N.E. Corner of the Orchard. In order to get within bombing distance it was necessary for them to crawl about 15 yards across the open after leaving the disused trench as they could only get by means of the latter to within about 30 yards of the Germans.

The bombs appeared to cause considerable consternation among some Germans round a fire though it was of course impossible to tell what damage was done.

The Germans opened rapid fire on our two bombers who however regained the cover of the disused trench safely.

We had one Rifleman wounded by a stray bullet after dark near WINDY CORNER and also one of the stretcher bearers who was carrying this man down from our dressing station to the Field Ambulance was hit by another.

19th. During the morning 2nd Lieut. Fisher with a party of Riflemen lately trained in the use of the trench mortar fired several shots from one of the latter from near the WHITE HOUSE barricade: several shells

FEB^Y.   40

appeared to fall either in or close to the
German trenches.
In the afternoon the Germans replied by
shelling the front of SCOTTISH TRENCH with
high explosive shells apparently searching
for the trench mortar, no damage was done
by them.
In the evening 2nd Lieut. Hoare was wounded
in the foot while standing near the road
RESERVE House in which his platoon was
billeted: this was apparently due to a
stray bullet.
'A' and 'B' Coys. were relieved in the trenches
by 'C' and 'D' in the afternoon.
Fine but cold and windy day.
Casualties - 1 Rifleman wounded.

20th. During the morning Lieut. Fisher fired 12
shots from the trench mortar near the WHITE
HOUSE apparently into the German trenches
opposite SCOTTISH TRENCH. The Germans
replied by shelling the RED HOUSE and Sunk
road with 4 inch howitzers without however
doing any damage to the party with the
trench mortar which had just finished
firing when the German shelling began.
At 5.20 p.m a party of stormers of Staffs.
and Berks. after artillery preparation
rushed a portion of the German trench

Feb?

a little way to our right opposite a part of the line known as the "Ducks Bill".
The chief object of this exploit was to discover whether the Germans had started a mine towards our trenches at this point.
No mine was discovered and the party got back successfully to their own trenches.
The German artillery reply to our guns appeared very feeble.
Casualties - One Rifleman wounded.

21st. Very foggy morning. Fog cleared about 11 a.m. Extraordinarily quiet day. Very little sniping and practically no shelling.
After the heavy rain the previous afternoon the trenches were rather wet underfoot.
About dusk 'C' and 'D' Coys. were relieved in the trenches by 'A' and 'B'.
Casualties - NIL.

22nd. Very foggy all day.
There was consequently very little shelling or sniping.
During the night one Rifleman of 'A' Coy. was killed by a sniper while on the look out.
1 Rifleman Killed.

23rd. Quiet day.
Lieut. Col. H.R. Green, Commanding 7th Battalion arrived for attachment for 4 days.

FEB?

Foggy morning but fog lifted in the afternoon.
In the evening 'A' and 'B' Coys. were relieved in the trenches by 'C' and 'D'.
Casualties - NIL.

24th. Wet morning but finer in the afternoon. About 10.15 p.m. 'D' Coy. who had located a German working party to their left front (apparently putting up new breastworks) opened a burst of rapid fire from their trenches and also fired a machine gun. It was of course impossible to say with what result.
Casualties - NIL.

25th. In the morning the ground was covered with snow and more fell at intervals but by the afternoon it had nearly all thawed.
The melting snow of course made the trenches very wet.
At 3 p.m. a Coy. of the 5th (Kings) Liverpool Regt. (Territorials) arrived; they were to be attached to the battalion for 48 hours to learn trench work and 1 platoon of them went with both 'A' and 'B' Coys. into the trenches when the two latter went up to relieve 'C' and 'D' in the evening.

FEB.Y

'A' Coy. when relieving 'C' in addition also took over the barricade on the road at FRENCH FARM from the Berks. and the small part of SCOTTISH TRENCH previously held by that regiment also the post at the RED HOUSE at the corner of the ORCHARD.
Casualties - one Rifleman wounded.

26th. Foggy and cold morning.
During the afternoon 2nd Lieut. Fisher fired three bombs from the TRENCH MORTAR into the enemy's trenches opposite Scottish Trench.
About 5-30 p.m. the enemy's artillery were more active than they had been for some time, shelling GIVENCHY with fairly big howitzers firing "common shell". Three shells fell in 'B' Coy. trenches one of which killed one Rifleman and wounded Sgt. Elliott: this occurred just as the two platoons of the 5th. Ing's were being relieved by the other two platoons of their Company, and as the latter were close to where the shells fell they were lucky not to have any casualties.
About 11 p.m. the enemy opened a burst of rapid fire apparently directed at a working party of the Berks. on our right, who were digging in very strong moonlight, in front of their trenches.

27th. Very cold morning and windy.

FEBY.

During the morning 2nd Lieut. Else and I climbed up into the upper part of WHITE HOUSE and I took 8 photographs of the German trenches of which an excellent view was obtainable.

A second line of trenches was visible about 70 yards behind the German front line, this second line appeared very strong being loopholed chiefly with iron plate loopholes and protected by a second line of chevaux de frise in addition to wire.

The front line (visible from our trenches) seemed only to be used for sniping and observation purposes, its parapet too, being very high completely screened the second line from view.

There appeared to be no parados to the front line into the back of which consequently the enemy could fire in case of its capture by us.

In the evening 'A' and 'B' Coys. were relieved in the trenches by 'C' and 'D'. (the two latter changing over from their usual trenches)

28th. Very fine sunny day.
During the morning Colonel MacMaster (5th Kings Territorials) went round our trenches and visited his men who were

FEBY.

attached to us.
In the afternoon news came that Colonel Northey had been given command of the 15th Brigade (5th Division).

RECONNAISSANCE REPORT OF 27.2.15 & MAP.

COPY of Report from Lt Col NORTHEY
re reconnaissance made by Captain
W.A.C. SAUNDERS KNOX-GORE and 2nd Lt ELSE (H)
on 27-2-15.

x x x x x x

It being most important that we should know where the enemy's true defensive line is, and what is behind it; and owing to the shape of the ground, it being impossible to see behind their front trenches, these two officers crept up into the skeleton roof of the ruined WHITE HOUSE, 150' from the enemy. 2nd Lt ELSE sketched the German position; copy herewith. Captain Knox-Gore took eight photographs which I am getting developed. It was a dangerous job and I watched it with anxiety: A German sniper spotted them, but fortunately did not hit them. The information is invaluable, making it clear that in front of WHITE HOUSE and ORCHARD the enemy's front-trench is hardly held, only used for sniping and observation, but that they have a very strong loopholed line of defence 100 yards or less behind. Their front line has no "parados" and would be a trap to an assaulting column (party), who on gaining the front line of trenches would be under the unexpected, heavy, fire of the second or real line. The front line is little more than a breastwork as far as can be seen — The photographs should be most useful. x x x x x x x x x x x x x x

27th Feb
15/

(sd) Edward Northey, Col
Cmdg 1st K.R.R.

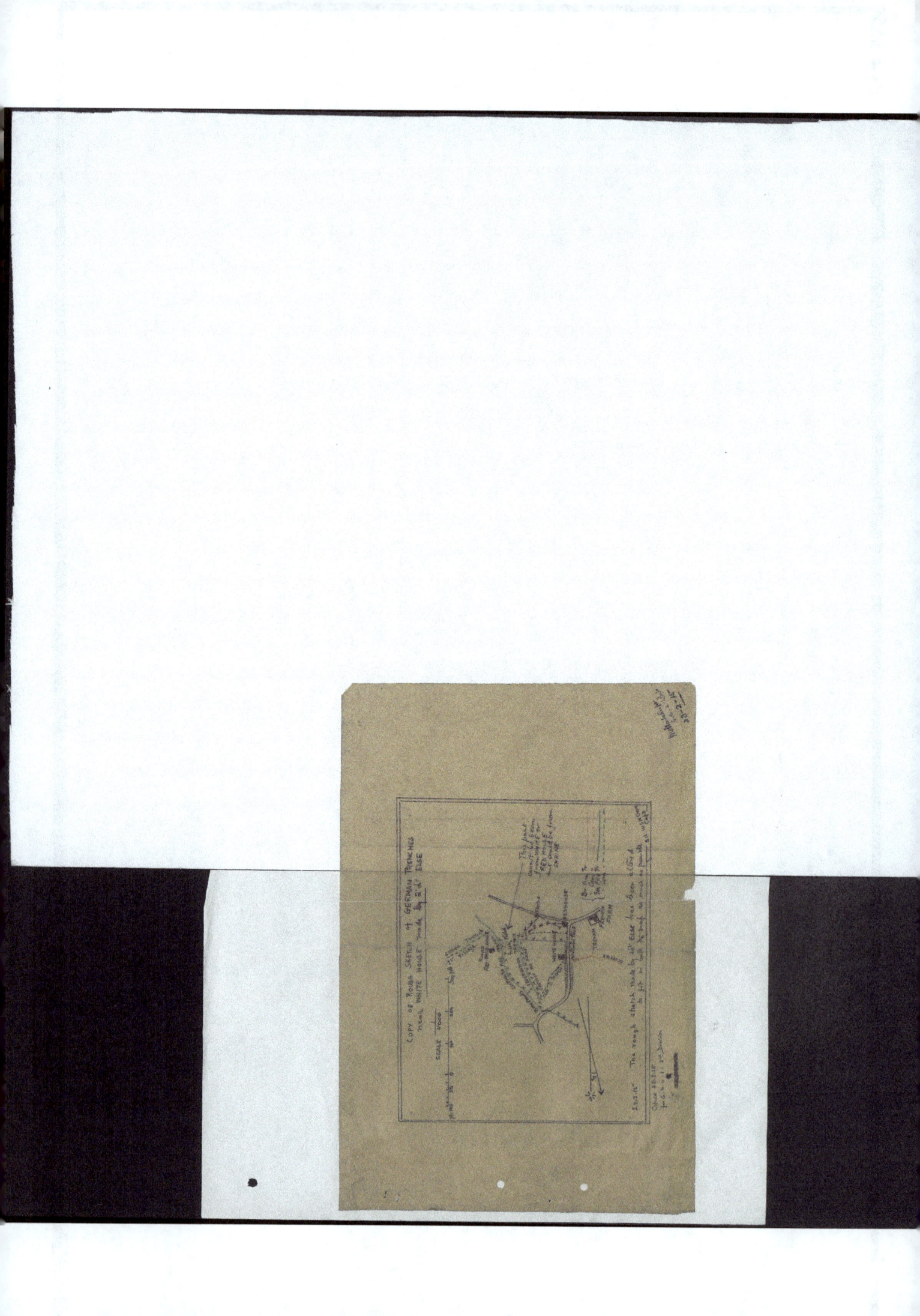

COPY

6th Infantry Brigade.
2nd Division.

WAR DIARY

1st BATTN. THE KING'S ROYAL RIFLE CORPS.

MARCH

1915

COPY OF 1/60th DIARY.

1915.

Mch. 1st.   About 7.30 a.m. H.R.H. The Prince of Wales walked round the trenches occupied by the Battalion with General Horne. and was much interested in everything.

[as] quite a heavy

relieved in the

left to take

[comman]d of the Battalion.

relieved in the

[bee]n awarded D.C.M.

[a]t Givenchy and

ordered to take

10th.

MARCH

1st. About 7.30 a.m. H.R.H. The Prince of Wales walked round the trenches occupied by the Battalion with General Horne, and was much interested in everything.
A fine sunny morning but later there was quite a heavy shower of snow.
In the evening 'C' and 'D' Coys. were relieved in the trenches by 'A' and 'B'.
Casualties - 1 Rfn. Killed.

2nd. Fine sunny day.
At 9.30 a.m. Brigadier Genl. Northey, left to take command of the 15th Brigade.
Major Shakerley, D.S.O. assumed command of the Battalion.

3rd. Quiet day.
In the evening 'A' and 'B' Coys. were relieved in the trenches by 'C' and 'D'.

COPY OF 1/60th DIARY.

1915.

Mch. 1st.   About 7.30 a.m. H.R.H. The Prince of Wales walked round the trenches occupied by the Battalion with General Horne, and was much interested in everything.

A fine sunny morning but later there was quite a heavy shower of snow.

In the evening "C" and "D" Coys. were relieved in the trenches by "A" and "B".

Casualties - 1 Rifleman killed.

2nd.   Fine sunny day.

At 9.30 a.m. Brigadier General Northey left to take command of the 15th Brigade.

Major Shakerley, D.S.O. assumed command of the Battalion.

3rd.   Quiet day.

In the evening "A" and "B" Coys. were relieved in the trenches by "C" and "D".   6444 L/C. Hilton awarded D.C.M.

Capt: Grazebrook rejoined the Battalion.

4th)
5th)   Battalion continued to hold trenches at Givenchy and
6th)   made preparations for an offensive movement ordered to take
7th)
8th)   place about the 10th March.
9th)

10th.

Copy of 1/60th Diary (contd)

1915.

Mch. 10th.   Brigade ordered to assault German trenches after artillery bombardment. Battalion ordered to find two assaulting columns both of which were to form up in the sunk road near White House.

The right column ("A" Coy) under Captain Willan was to advance with its right on the northern hedge of the orchard and attack the German second line of trenches which ran from opposite the N.W. corner of the Orchard northwards. The left column ("C" Coy) under Major Armytage was to assault the German trenches just South of an at the top of "The Bluff."

Both assaulting Coys. were arranged as follows: Two platoons in the first line, one platoon in the second and one in the third.

The two leading platoons of "A" Coy. were under Captain Shakerley, the platoon commanders being 2nd Lieut. Crawhall (on right) and 2nd Lieut. Birkett (on left).

The second line consisted of 2nd Lieut. Else's platoon, and the third 2nd Lieut. Fisher's. "C" Coy. (on left) had 2nd Lieut. Fellowe's platoon (right) and 2nd Lieut. Ward's platoon (left) in the front line with whom was Capt. Grazebrook. In the second line was 2nd Lieut. Harron's platoon, 2nd Lieut. Steadman's forming the third. The second line was closely followed by 2nd Lieut. Slater with two machine guns, and 2nd Lieut. Parsons, R.E. with a trench blocking party advanced between the first and second lines of this Coy. The assault was timed to take place at 8.10 a.m. The artillery began registering on the enemy's wire at 7 a.m. The artillery bombardment began at 7.30 a.m., and lasted for 10 minutes. From 7.38 to 7.41 a.m. covering fire was kept up by 5th King's (Territorials) and Machine Guns from the left part of Scottish Trench.   "B" Coy.

1915.
Mch. 10th
(contd).

"B" Coy. (Captain Bonham Carter) was ordered closely to follow "C" Coy. and support it. At 7.50 a.m. the second artillery bombardment was begun and continued on the enemy's trenches until 8.10 a.m. at which time the artillery lengthened their range and the assault took place.

At 7.55 a.m. the assaulting Coys. began to get out to their assaulting positions in the sunk road. "A" Coy. and one platoon of "C" moving by the barricade on the road near French Farm and the rest of "C" Coy. by the white House sap. "B" Coy. followed "A" by the barricade.

At 8.10 a.m. both assaulting parties having assembled on the White House road endeavoured to rush the enemy's trenches about 170 yards away.

The right party advanced at the double over the intervening ground and soon came under a heavy fire (rifle and machine gun) losing many casualties, those remaining continued their advance but when within about 30 yards of the wire entanglement were almost annihilated by cross machine gun fire. Some men threw themselves on the ground as they could not get through the entanglement which had nowhere been breeched and which consisted of trestles and high wire entanglement. Only a very small number of men succeeded in reaching the wire and none got into the enemy's trench.

The left party advanced at the double and some of them succeeded in getting into the enemy's trench notwithstanding many casualties and I believe some of them penetrated as far as the enemy's support trench, but it is impossible to say with certainty as only from one party has anyone returned. The wire had not been breeched but this party succeeded in crawling through it and established themselves in the enemy's front trench by blocking the latter in two places

and also

1915.
Mch. 10th.
(contd).

and also a communication trench leading towards the support trench.

This party maintained their position in the enemy's front trench in spite of heavy rifle fire and bomb throwing till nearly 2 p.m. by which time only one sergeant and two Riflemen remained unwounded and they then succeeded in crawling back to our lines making use of what had once been a communication trench. Sergeant Robinson who had been with this party had succeeded in getting back along this route about 11 a.m. to report the situation there. There were two officers (Captain Grazebrook and 2nd Lieut. Ward) two sergeants (Sergent Robinson and Sergeant Crooks) and 10 Riflemen in this party and both officers were wounded quite e early in the morning, but apparently both inside the German trench.

The supporting parties which were sent to assist this party were practically wiped out by fire, rifle and machine gun.

The two machine guns in charge of 2nd Lieut. R.H.Slater accompanied the left party and they succeeded in getting quite close to the wire entanglement, 5 of the detachment were shot but in spite of this 2nd Lieut. Slater succeeded in getting back both guns to our lines, himself going out a second time to assist in getting in one gun which had been left out. Both of the assaulting parties started at exactly the right moment, followed out their orders perfectly, and if gallantry and determination could have commanded success it would have been theirs. No more gallant exploit could be seen. Notwithstanding a heavy rifle and machine gun cross fire they rushed on and those who got near the wire were unable to get through as nowhere had it been breached.

After dark

1915.
Mch. 10th.
(contd).

After dark relief parties were organized under 2nd Lieut Fisher to bring in wounded and about 35 were brought in. A few unwounded succeeded in crawling in as well, among these was 2nd Lieut. Birkett (3rd Somersets attached) -who had lain all day in a shell hole close to the enemy's wire. He had a terrible experience as all day if he made the least movement he was at once fired on at close range by the Germans and during our second artillery bombardment from 2.15 to 2.45 p.m. the Lyddite shells from our Field and Siege howitzers were falling all round him.

2nd Lieut. Else who had been right among the enemy's wire, succeeded in crawling back during this bombardment although wounded in four placed.

The casualties for the day were as follows:-

	Missing but believed killed	Killed.	Wounded.		
"A" Coy.	65.		44.	=	109.
"B" "	7.	6.	8.	=	21.
"C" "	46.	28.	42.	=	116.
"D" "	1 (Mg)			=	1.
					247.

Besides the above we had the following casualties among officers:-

(1) Captain E.P.Shakerley, killed.
(2) Captain C.A.Grazebrook, wounded and missing.
(3) 2nd Lieut.F.P.Crawhall, believed killed.
(4) 2nd Lieut.H.Else, wounded.
(5) Lieut.P.J.Bevan, believed killed.
(6) 2nd Lieut.A.R.Herron, believed killed.
(7) 2nd Lieut.R.Fellowes, believed killed.
(8) 2nd Lieut.K.Ward, wounded and missing. Subsequently unofficially reported prisoner of War.

Only the leading ½ platoon of "B" Coy. actually took part in the assault (Lieut.Bevan's), and this ½ platoon only got about 30 yards from the White House road. The remainder of "B" Coy. was stopped and also the last platoon of "A"

1915.
Mch. 10th.
(contd) of "A" when it was seen what had occurred to the parties which had started earlier.

A second assault, in which, however, the Battalion was not to take place, was ordered to be made by the King's and S.Staffs. at 2.45 p.m. after a second artillery bombardment. The Battalion was ordered to assist this second assault by fire and make use of any opportunity to advance which offered itself. As the bombardment did not however, breach the enemy's wire, this second assault did not take place and the Battalion moved down for the night to its old billets at Windy Corner leaving the 5th King's Regiment supported by 2 platoons of "B" Coy to hold Scottish Trench and New Cut.

Copy of 1/60th diary.

1915.
Mch. 11th.

6th Brigade ordered to re-assume the offensive. The 1st Berks. were ordered to assault the German trenches South of the Orchard and "D" Coy. were to be held in readiness to support them. The assault was to be preceded by a deliberate artillery preparation designed firstly to destroy the enemy's machine gun position at the N.E. corner of the Orchard and secondly to breach their wire South of that point. Owing to the fact that the artillery did not succeed in making sufficient gaps in the wire the attack was cancelled. In the evening the 6th Brigade were relieved in the trenches by the 4th (Guards) Brigade.

The Battalion handed over its trenches to the 1st Herts. (Territorials). The Coys. on relief marched independently via Le Preol and Beuvry to Bethune where they went into billets in the Tobacco Factory, the last Company arriving shortly before midnight.

Casualties - 2 wounded.

12th.

Brigade in Corps Reserve. About 2.30 p.m. news was received that the 7th Division had broken through the enemy's lines at Moulin le Pietre and the Brigade was ordered to be ready to move at the shortest notice.

During the morning General Fanshawe visited the Battalion in their billets and expressed his satisfaction on the work done by it on the 10th.

Brigade kept ready to move at short notice all night.

6 o.r. joined.

13th.

Brigade remained in billets in Bethune. In the evening a draft of 60 N.C.O's and Riflemen arrived and were all posted to "A" Coy.

14th.

Copy of 1/60th Diary.

1915.
Mch. 14th.   Battalion attended church parade at the theatre Bethune. After the service the battalion was addressed by General Horne commanding 2 Division who congratulated them on the splendid attack carried out on the 10th. He said that although the German trenches had not been captured and held by the 6th Brigade, we were not to think for a moment that we had failed in our object. Our first object had been to contain the enemy near Givenchy and prevent them detaching troops to fight our main attack at Neuve Chapelle. This the Brigade had been entirely successful in doing. The second object had been the capture of the German trenches at Givenchy. Ad if this object had not bee attained it was through no fault of the Brigades, who had done all that was humanly possible. 2nd Lt. Bushell to England on sick leave.

15th.   Brigade remained in billets in Bethune. Concert given by Battalion and S.Staffs. in theatre Bethune

16th.   General Sir C.Monroe commanding 1st Corps visited the Battalion in billets and congratulated them on the attack made near Givenchy on 10th.

17th.   Following Temporary 2nd Lieut's from cadet school Bailleul joined Battalion. Posted to Coys. as follows:

        L.E.Hall.   "A" Coy.
        L.F.Taylor.   "A" "
        J.S.H.James.   "B" "
        C.E.Hardy.   "C" "
        K.J.B.Addey.   "C" "
        F.N.Parker.   "D" "

18th.   Brigade remained in billets at Bethune.

19th.   Ditto.
2nd Lt. Grenville Grey & 80 o.r. joined.

20th.

Copy of 1/60th diary.

1915.

Mch. 20th.   C.O.Coy. Commanders and self motored (in car lent by 2nd Div) to inspect new line to be taken over by Battalion near Cuinchy. Fine but cold day. In evening orders were received that 6th Brigade was to relieve 5th next day instead of on 22nd.

21st.   6th Brigade relieved 5th Brigade in Cuinchy line. Battalion left Bethune (Coys. at intervals of 20 minutes) at 2 p.m. and marched via Beuvry to Cuinchy. Two companies of the 6th King's Liverpool Regiment (Territorials) were attached to the Battalion and put under the command of the C.O. These two companies, and "B" and "D" Coys. of the Battalion took over the trenches from the 2nd Ox. and Bucks. Light Infantry.

The companies were distributed as follows:-

On the right connecting with the French on the La Bassee - Bethune road was "C" Coy. 5th King's; these occupied the fire trench known as Waterloo Place and half of Seymour Street. In support of them was "A" Coy. of the same Battalion in Praed Street and part of Edgware Road. On the left "D" Coy. 1st K.R.Rifles held the remainder of Seymour street connecting with the 1st R.Berks. just in front of a brick stack known as the Cock Shy. "D" Coy. were supported by "B" who occupied the Keep and the supporting trenches near it.

On the La Bassee road the German trenches were about 250 yards away while opposite the Cock Shy they were only about 60 yards.

The Battalion Headquarters was in the house in Cuinchy we had occupied just before Xmas but since then the house had been much knocked about and there was only one room with the exception of the cellars which had not been wrecked by shells.

21st. (contd)

Copy of 1/60th diary.

1915.
Mch. 21st.
(contd).   Quiet night. Rapid fire was opened at 1 a.m. at the request of the French to assist some opernations they were carrying out to the South of us.

22nd.   Beautiful sunny day, and quite warm. Germans fired a few shells about the houses in Cuinchy but did no damage. Quiet night. No casualties but one man of 5th King's killed.

23rd.   Fine but cloudy day. About 8 a.m. Germans put a few small shells behind our Headquarters and dressing station. Enemy's artillery rather more active all day. Rain started about 4.30 p.m.

During the afternoon a redistrubition of the Coys. in the trenches was carried out. "B" Coy. 1st K.R.Rifles took over the fire trench with its right on the La Bassee road. "D" Coy. 1st K.R.Rifles moved into Praed Street as right supporting Company but left one platoon to garrison the Keep. The 5th King's took over the fire trench formerly held by "D" Coy. and put their supporting company in the support trenches near the Keep.

News was received that 2nd Lieut H.Else had been awarded the Military Cross.

Major Haig 6th R.B. transferred to Welsh Guards.

24th.   Wet day. A good deal of water in the trenches.
After dark a new communication trench was dug east of the church connecting Old Kent Road and Hertford Street.

25th.   Battalion relieved in trenches by 2nd S.Staffs. Coys, moved independently into Bethune Tobacco Factory. Battalion ordered to form Divisional Reserve.

26th.

Copy of 1/60th diary (contd).

1915.
Mch. 26th.   Battalion remained in billets in Bethune in Divisional reserve.

27th.   Ditto.   Sergeant McClellan awarded D.C.Medal. 72 o.r. joined.

28th.   Motored to Reninghelst to see 3rd and 4th Battalions who were in billets near there.

29th.   Battalion relieved S.Staffords in trenches at Cuinchy (A1 section). "A" Coy. took over the fire trench (Waterloo Place and Seymour Street). "C" Coy. (temporarily under Capt. Pauley) were in support in Praed Street. 2 platoons of "D" Coy under Lieut. Alston garrisoned the Keep. The trenches were quite dry and a certain amount of new dug-outs had been made also a new redoubt on the La Bassee road at the end of Praed Street.

Major Armytage went to hospital having hurt his knee. Sergeant McClellan wounded.

30th.   Fine but cold morning. Very quiet but enemy's artillery rather more active in the afternoon.

During the day we fired a few bombs from the catapult at the German brick stacks.

31st.   Another fine sunny day, enemy's artillery again rather active. The 7th King's Liverpool Regt. (Territorials) completed a new communication trench to be known as Seventh Street running from Hertford Street to the junction of Praed Street and Marylebone Road. This gave us a new and considerably shorter route from No. 1 Harley Street to our trenches.

COPY

6th Infantry Brigade.
2nd Division.

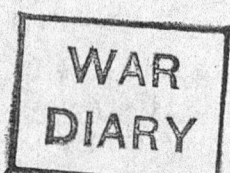

1st BATTN. THE KING'S ROYAL RIFLE CORPS.

A P R I L

1 9 1 5

COPY OF 1/60th DIARY.

1915.
April 1st.

In view of the fact that it was Bismarck's birthday and in order to afford the Brigade practice in forming up for an attack or counter-attack -

The Brigade reserves &c were moved up into cover trenches in the neighbourhood of Cuinchy.

"B" and "D" Coys. were brought up from Annequin at 5 a.m and moved into a cover trench just in rear of the artillery observation post on the Cuinchy - Cambrin Road and into Marylebone Road respectively. At 9 a.m. all being quiet, these two Coys were ordered to return to their billets in Annequin.

During the afternoon the enemy dropped about 25 big howitzer shells near our Battalion Headquarters. Among them were seven consecutive "blinds". No damage whatever was done. During the evening the construction of an Advanced Battalion Headquarters was begun at Machine Gun House and also 6 saps started from Seymour Street in the direction of the German trenches. These were begun as mines and were to come up above ground in front of our parapet.

2nd.   Another fine sunny day.

In the afternoon "D" and "B" Coys relieved "C" and "A" in the trenches. During the night fire was opened on

the

Copy of 1/60th diary.

1915.
April 2nd (contd)

the German trenches at intervals by machine guns (using indirect fire from near the Pont Fixe Road) and also by 2nd Lieut. Parker with the Trench Mortars. Sniping was also kept up constantly.

3rd. Dull and rather misty morning. The Brigade having been ordered to make a feint attack. From 4 a.m. sniping fire was kept up by all our front line until 4.50 a.m. The 4th Guards Brigade at Givenchy also opened a burst of raid fire at daybreak.

From 4.50 a.m. to 5 a.m. very heavy fire was opened on enemy's trenches by rifles and machine guns, firing indirect.

All fire ceased from 5 to 5.5 a.m. and at that hour our first mine was exploded followed after an interval of about half a minute by the second. Both explosions threw up great masses of earth and debris, and gave out clouds of white smoke but curiously enough they made v. little noise. After the smoke had cleared away it was seen that about 100 yards of the enemy's front trench just in front of their nearest brick stacks had been demolished. The front of one of these brick stacks had been blown away and this disclosed a sniper's gallery apparently running right through the brick stack and supported by wooden beams. A German who was inside at the time was plainly visible buried up to his waist in debris and hanging out of the ruined front of the brick stack. It is of course impossible to say whether the enemy's trench was strongly held at the moment of the explosion but a few hours afterwards, shovelfuls of earth were to be seen being thrown up by the enemy who had obviously started to repair the damage.

About 8.30 a.m. the Battalion having been relieved by the S.Staffs. in the trenches moved back into billets in the Tobacco Factory at Bethune, Capt. Saunders Knox Gore went to Brigade Headquarters to do Brigade Major for 5 days while Kelly was on leave.

4th. Battalion remained in billets in Bethune in Divisional Reserve.

5th. Ditto.

6th. Ditto. About 11.40 p.m. Orders were received by Battalion to stand to arms owing to an attempt by the enemy to blow up part of the French trenches on our right just South of the La Bassee road and also the explosion of two mines just in front of the centre of the section of our line held by the 5th Liverpools. However, 10 minutes later the order "to stand to arms" was cancelled as information had been received that the enemy's mines had done no damage having exploded some distance in front of our trenches.

7th. Battalion remained in billets in Bethune in Divisional Reserve until 1 p.m. when they marched to Cuinchy and relieved the S.Staffs. in the trenches. "B" Coy. taking over the fire trenches and "D" the supporting trenches. "A" and "C" moved into billets in Tourbieres taking them over from the 7th Liverpools.

A good deal of rain during the night which was very quiet.
8th.

Copy of 1/60th diary. (contd)

1915.
April 8th.   Very quiet morning. Some shelling during the afternoon.
Fine day with a drying wind which dried up the trenches
which had been very wet. Snipers Alley bombed during
night.
        Casualties -
    Heard that 2nd Lieut. Slater had been given Military
Cross and Capt: Saunders Knox Gore awarded D.S.O.

9th.   Some shelling of our trenches during the day, during
which there were hail showers and also some rain. During
the afternoon "B" and "D" Coys. were relieved in the
trenches by "A" and "C" respectively. About 8 p.m. 2nd
Lieut. France with two men worked his way up an old communication trench leading towards the enemy's trenches. They
found a loopholed barricade blocking it which they destroyed. They then went 15 yards further and lay down for about
an hour in the hope of catching a German, but as no one
appeared they threw 4 bombs towards the enemy and got back
safely.

10th.   At 4 a.m. the French exploded a mine under the German
trenches about 200 yards South of the La Bassee road, des-
troying a German countermine, and a considerable portion of
their front trench. After the explosion the French guns,
our 16th Battery and 2nd Lieut Parker (with trench mortars)
opened fire on the German trenches. The Germans replied
with rapid rifle fire and a few shells mostly near Cuinchy
supporting point. Between 9 and 11 a.m. the enemy fired
about 60 large high explosive shells (probably 6 inch) in
the neighbourhood of Cuinchy Church. Very little damage wa
done by them (except to the church!).   About 11.30 a.m.,
our 56th Battery fired on the enemy's brick stacks, apparently with good effect. Quiet night.

11th.   Fine sunny morning. Kelly having returned I went back
to Battalion headquarters at Cuinchy. During the afternoon
Battalion was relieved in the trenches by the 2nd S.Staffs.
and moved back to billets in the Tobacco Factory in Bethune
in Divisional Reserve.   On arrival a draft of 53 N.C.Os and
men joined the Battalion.

12th.   Fine day but cold. Battalion remained in Bethune in
Division Reserve.

13th.   Battalion remained in Division Reserve.

14th.   Ditto.

15th.   Fine sunny morning. Battalion left Bethune about 1.15
p.m. marched to Cuinchy and relieved S.Staffs in the trenches
"D" Coy. (Lieut.Alston) in the front trenches and "B" in
support.
    An extraordinarily quiet afternoon and evening hardly
a shot being fired.

                                16th.

Copy of 1/60th diary (contd).

1915.
April 16th.   About 3 a.m. the Germans exploded 3 mines two in front of the French trenches South of the La Bassee road and one opposite the left of the line held by "D" Coy. All these mines were a considerable distance from our trenches and did no damage. During the night "D" Coy.and also the 5th Liverpools on our left opened bursts of fire in the hope of catching the enemy putting wire on some new posts which had been observed opposite Waterloo Place.

At about 7.45 a.m. the enemy began quite a heavy artillery bombardment with both light guns and also 5.9" Howitzers. They seemed to fire without any particular object sending their shells indiscriminately over our trenches, Cuinchy and the Pont Fixe road. The bombardment lasted about half an hour and then ceased altogether.

Whether the cessation was due to our guns which had begun to fire a few rounds it was impossible to say, as was the reason for this sudden show of activity on the enemy's part. Possibly it was meant as an indication that bursts of fire at intervals during the night were not appreciated. At any rate the enemy wasted some hundreds of shells without doing any appreciable damage.   Quiet night.

17th.   About 7.30 a.m. Germans began a quite heavy bombardment of our front trenches with large high explosive Howitzer shells and also with light shrapnel. Beyond completely blocking Regent Street and burying two Riflemen of "B" Coy in a dug-out (one of whom died of suffocation) no damage was done, the front of the parapet in Seymour Street was also rather knocked about. The shelling lasted about half an hour. The rest of the morning was fairly quiet. About 3 p.m. the enemy suddenly began to shell the Keep with shrapnel and caught 2nd Lieut. France, hitting him in the leg but not dangerously. They also unluckily caught Sergeant Hilyard of the Machine Gun Section who was going up Old Kent Road killing him instantly.

About 4 p.m., they turned their attention (and the 6" howitzer) on to our Headquarter house without doing any damage. They fired about 12 shells at it, 4 of which were "blinds", they appeared to come from the direction of Canteleux. One of them filled the cellar in which the signallers were with dust and smoke. The Germans also fired their new Minenwerfer during the evening at the neighbourhood of the Keep.

Casualties for day - 2 Killed, 2nd Lieut. Hayhurst France and 2 Riflemen wounded.

18th.   Quiet night and beautiful sunny morning. Enemy did not give us the early morning bombardment which they had done the last few days. About 10.30 a.m., they fired 3 shells at our Headquarter house, this may have been the result of the reconnaissance of a German aeroplane which came over about 10 a.m., at which hour the Headquarter signallers were engaged on their morning task of lighting their brazier and showing as much smoke as possible! The aeroplane cleared off on being fired at by the anti-aircraft guns and by rifles and the shells did no harm but were pretty close, one small piece coming into our dining room through the wall.

During the afternoon the enemy(s Minenwerfer opened fire from just on the North side of the La Bassee road, but soon stopped after our artillery had fired a few rounds in that part of the world. During the night "D" Coy. sent two platoons up from Tourbieres to dig a new trench to replace Regent Street which was damaged beyond repair and also to make two new dug-outs near Machine Gun House to accommodate

some of our

Copy of 1/60th diary (contd).

1915.
April 18th.
(contd) some of our Headquarters which had been ordered to move up there owing to a new redistribution of the Brigade line which from the next day was to be divided into 4 sub-sections instead of 3. They also continued digging out a new Machine Gun House connecting Marylebone Road with the latter, they unluckily had a man killed by a stray bullet while doing this job.

19th. Beautiful morning and quite the warmest day we have had this year. About 9.20 a.m. a German Biplane came over our lines flying very high, but made off at once when fired on by rifles. About 12 noon the 6th London (T) arrived to take over our Headquarters which was to become the Headquarters of sub-section A3 in future. About 1.30 p.m. we moved up to our new Headquarters at Machine Gun House taking most of our furniture &c. with us. The two dug-outs there will be very comfortable, we have one for eating and living in and one to sleep in. Our telephones were installed in the small cellar under the house. We are making two new dug-outs as well, one for the officers servants and one for the ammunition, bombs, &c. About 2.45 p.m. some of the parapet of Seymour Street, was blown in by a Minenwerfer, and one Rifleman was killed by a shell which came in through the gap a few seconds later. The Battalion was relieved in the trenches about 4 p.m. by the S.Staffords and moved back to Bethune into Divisional Reserve.

20th. Fine day. Battalion remained in Reserve.

21st. Ditto.

22nd. Ditto.

23rd. Ditto.

24th. Battalion left Bethune at 7 a.m. and marched to Cuinchy to relieve 2nd S.Staffs. in sub-section A1. "B" Coy. took over the fire trench and "D" the supporting trenches and Keep. "A" and "C" Coys. moved into their old billets in Tourbieres. On arrival we found that the Stafford's Headquarters had been shelled out of their new Headquarters at Machine Gun House. We found them installed in our old dressing station and we decided to use that as our headquarters until the house in Willow Road (which we had been ordered to move to eventually) had been made habitable by the R.E.
During the morning the enemy did a good deal of indiscriminate shelling with whizz-bangs, and also shelled our late Headquarters (near the Berkshires) with big shells.
About 11.20 a.m. they hit the dressing station three times in a few seconds. They wounded 5 of the Headquarters including the Adjutants orderly Harrington. The latter however, remained at duty. One small piece came into our sitting room.
About 4 p.m., our 6 inch seige Howitzers shelled the enemy's brick stacks and this apparently stirred them up and made them do a certain amount of shelling with whizz-bangs which they kept up even after dark. About 8 p.m. heavy rifle fire was audible from the direction of Givenchy.

During the

Copy of 1/60th diary.

1915.
April 24th.
(contd).
During the evening owing to the reported use near Languemarck by the enemy of asphyxiating gasses every man in the trenches was fitted with an improvised mask made out of field dressings. These masks were to be dipped if necessary with a solution of bicarbonate of soda which was stored in rum jars at intervals along the trenches.

The enemy having continued intermittent shelling till nearly 10 p.m. and hit the dressing station again remained quiet for the rest of the night. It rained steadily most of the night.

25th.
Dull, cloudy morning but the rain had ceased. Unusually quiet morning during which the enemy did hardly any shelling. About 3 p.m. they began to shell our Headquarters at the dressing station again. They fired about 20 shells, hit the wall once but did no harm. After quarter of an hour the shelling ceased.

During the afternoon we moved our Headquarters down to Woburn Abbey (on Willow Road) the R.E. had not finshed work on the house but we moved in for the night. A good deal of transport was heard moving during the early part of the night in the direction of Auchy. A white dog (possibly a spy's dog) crossed our trenches about 9 p.m. on the L Bassee road and went along the road to the German lines. This dog returned at 1 a.m. it was fired at but missed. It went down in the direction of Annequin.

26th.
Nice warm sunny morning. Quiet morning, enemy fired a few Minenwerfers at our trenches but did little damage.

R.E. continued work on Woburn Abbey all day, sandbagging the roof, glazing the window, &c. During the afternoon a good deal of artillery fire was audible in the distance both North and South of us but a long way off. About 7 p.m. there was rapid rifle fire in the direction of Givenchy and North of it. The enemy also began shelling Givenchy with 8 inch Howitzers and three mines were seen to explode not far from the Church and there was a certain amount of shelling with light guns on the North side of the Canal.

Fairly quiet night but desultory firing in direction of Givenchy.

During the afternoon "D" and "B" Coys. had been relieved in the trenches by "A" & "C" respectively.

27th.
At 3.30 a.m. a test was carried out to discover how long it would take the artillery to open fire on their night lines. The 16th battery fired their first round $4\frac{3}{4}$ minutes after their observing officer who sleeps at our Headquarters was given the order to fire. Quiet and fine day, enemy did a little shelling with Whizz-bangs fired mostly in salvoes. During the afternoon a draft of 60 N.C.Os and Riflemen joined the Battalion.

Repairs to Woburn Abbey were completed by R.E. and dugouts close by finished.

Quiet night, this was rather unexpected as the 7th Liverpools on our left about 9 p.m. occupied the near edge of the large mine crater between our lines and the Germans, which it was thought would probably stir up the latter to activity.

28th.
Very hot day. Usual shelling with whizz-bangs and Minenwerfers. During morning 2nd Lieut. F.N.Parker was found in his room at Brigade Headquarters shot in the head by a revolver.

Copy of 1/60th diary.

1915.
April 28th.
(contd).   revolver. About 3 p.m. S.Staffords arrived to relieve us in the trenches. Colonel Davidson had returned and reassumed command of them from Lieut.Col. Routledge. The Battalion on relief marched into Bethune into billets in the Orphanage, "B" Coy. (for whom there was no room in the latter) going to the Tobacco Factory. On arrival we heard that 2nd Lieut. Parker had died of wounds in hospital.
         66 o.r. joined, & Lt. A.J.Austin Cartwell to ENGLAND.

29th.   Very hot day. Battalion remained in billets at Bethune. 2nd Lieut.Cassidy joined the Battalion from Artists Rifles.

30th.   Hot sunny day.   110 N.C.O's and Riflemen were inoculated against enteric. Battalion remained in billets at Bethune.

COPY. 6th Infantry Brigade.
2nd Division.

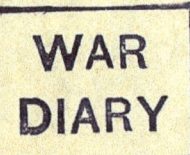

1st Battalion

KING'S ROYAL RIFLE CORPS.

MAY

1915.

COPY OF 1/60th DIARY.

1915.
May 1st.   Another very hot day. Owing to the heat permission
            was obtained from 6th Brigade for Battalion to carry out
            relief of S.Staffs, 2 hours later than usual. There was
            a good deal of shelling while the relief was taking
            place. It was finished by 6 p.m.   "D" Coy. took over
            the fire trench and "B" the support trench. Quiet night.

2nd.   Fine but cloudy morning. Unusually quiet all day.
            About 5 p.m. "C" and "A" Coys. relieved "D" and "B" in
            the trenches. During the evening very heavy artillery
            fire was audible to the North apparently about 12 miles
            away.
                During the night patrols were sent out to the front
            by "C" Coy. and while out Lieut.Donovan was wounded in
            the thigh; he managed however to get back into our
            trenches with the help of a Rifleman who was with him.

3rd.   Bright sunny morning but cold wind. Early in the
            afternoon the Germans bombarded the Keep heavily with a
            large trench mortar killing one Rifleman (the sentry on
            the look out for Minenwerfer bombs) and wounding one of the
            signallers in their dugouts.   Five rifles were complete-
            ly destroyed and 3 dug-outs damaged. The enemy were
            probably searching for our new (Vickers) trench mortar
            battery which had previously been firing from behind
            the Keep.
                During the day the 6th Brigade was relieved in
            Section A (Cuinchy) by the 5th Brigade. The Battalion
            was relieved in the trenches by the Inniskilling Fusiliers
            (Lieut.Colonel Wilding). The relief began at 5 p.m. but
            owing to some delay in the arrival of the Coy. to take
            over our support trenches it was not complete till 7.30
            p.m. and "A" Coy. did not get back to our billets in
            Faubourg D'Arras Bethune till about 10 p.m.

4th.   Battalion remained in billets in Bethune. Very hot
            day and heavy thunderstorm about 5 p.m.

5th.   Battalion marched out from billets at 10 a.m. and
            carried out practice in the assault, at Vertbois Farm
            about 2 miles North of Kinges. Very close day but misty.

6th.   Battalion marched out of billets at 7.55 a.m. to take
            part in Brigade Tactical Exercise near Vendin and return
            to billets about 2 p.m. Very hot muggy day.

7th.   Battalion remained in billets at Bethune. Very hot
            muggy day. Captain Hon.J.N.Bigge joined.

8th.   Battalion remained in billets at Bethune. Another hot
            muggy day. Secret orders had been issued over night
            that the Brigade was to move about 2 a.m. on 8th but these
            orders were cancelled the same evening.

9th.   Brigade ordered to move to neighbourhood of Le Touret
            in support of First Division. Battalion paraded at 1.15
            a.m. and moved to a farm at Le Touret arriving about 3.15
            a.m.
                Brigade remained for morning at Le Touret while the
            attack was being made by 1st Division on the Rue de Bois.
                                                            We heard

Copy of 1/60th diary.

1915.
May 9th.
(contd).

We heard during the morning that the 4th Corps had got into German line at Rouge Bancs but that assault by 1st Division had failed. About 3.10 p.m. the Battalion followed by 1st R.Berks (the two Battalions both under Major Shakerley) moved to Richebourg St. Vaast to support 1st Division who were to assault again at 4 p.m.

This assault also having failed the Battalion and Berks were ordered to move up to two lines of breastworks parallel to and just behind the Rue de Bois (this order was received about 5.30 p.m).

While the Battalion and the Berks were on their way to the breastworks further orders were received that the Battalion were to take over the trenches in front of the Rue de Bois from the South Wales Borderers and were to assault the German trenches in front of the latter at 8.30 p.m. The Berks were to take over the trenches on our right from the Gloucesters and assault in conjunction with us. At the time the above orders were received (soon after 7 p.m) only about one Coy. of the Battalion had reached the breastworks behind the Rue de Bois and the Berks were about half way between Richebourg and the latter. No time was available for proper reconnaissance oft the ground which was quite strange to us and it would hardly have been possible to get into a position to assault by 8.30 p.m. While hasty arrangements were being made and reconnoitring going on, the Brigade Mahor arrived in the trenches were were just taking over, with orders that we were to assault not only on our own front but on that allotted to the Berks as well as the latter could not possibly be in position in time. The C.O. was just on his way down about 8.20 p.m. to see the Brigadier and point out the impossibility of making the necessary arrangemens for the assault in time when a breathless officer arrived with the order that the assault was cancelled. The Battalion then settled down in its trenches "D" Coy. (right) and "B" (left) in the front line and "C" and "A" in breastworks behind "C" being in front of and "A" behind the Rue de Bois. "D" Coys right connected with the Berks and "B" Coys left with the 3rd Lond (Meerut Division). During the night we managed to get in a good many wounded most South Wales Borderers. Battalion Headquarters with those of Berks took over house from 3rd Brigade.

10th.

At 2.15 a.m. orders were received that the Battalion and Berks supported by 1st King's were to assault German trenches but not before 2 p.m. at earliest. All arrangements for the assault were however to be made before daylight. At 10 a.m. orders were received for 1st Corps that the assault was again cancelled. We had a good opportunity during the day of examining the ground attacked over by the 1st Division. This was quite flat and crossed by many ditches full of water.

There were three lines of breastworks in addition to the front line which was half breastwork, half trench.

These lines of breastworks all ran parallel to the Rue de Bois on about 100 yards in front and two behind it.

There was a ditch about 12 feet wide running along

small wooden

Copy of 1/60th diary.

1915.
May 10th.
(contd).. small wooden bridges placed there by the 1st Division for their assault. It was possible from the position of the dead to form a fairly good idea of what had happened during the 1st Division assault.

A very few were lying close up to the German trenches there were some at the bridges over the ditch 20 yds in front of our trenches and a good many just in front of our own parapet but the bast majority in our section of the line were lying scattered over the cultivated ground between our own 1st line trenches and the 2nd line of our breastworks. Why they had attempted to advance across open to get from our 2nd line up to our front line was not clear unless it was because of the extreme badness of the communications back from our front line. In our section a front of 400 yards there was only one communication trench and that not worthy of the name. It was in places only about a foot deep and in others its sides consisted of bits of canvas while at no point was it deeper than 4 feet while its average width must have been 5 or 6 feet. We had a fairly quiet day in the trenches having 5 casualties in all.

During the night our left Coys. trenches were taken over by the Gharwal Brigade and our right Coys by the H.L.I (5th Brigade). The Battalion moved back on relief to billets about Windy Corner about 500 yards behind the Rue due Bois the last Coy arriving there about 12 midnight.

11th. Battalion paraded at 6.10 a.m. and marched with remainder of Brigade (which had been ordered back to Divisional reserve) via Richbourg St.Vaast to billets just South of Lacouture. We spent a quiet morning there and were glad of a rest as although we had had no actual fighting we had been more or less "on the go" since 1 a.m. 9th May.

"B & "D" Coys especially who had been ordered to carry out the assault which had been cancelled had had a nerve trying time.

12th. Wet day which was rather unpleasant for "A" Coy who had no billets but had to bivouac in a field.

13th. About 5 p.m. Battalion moved off independently by Coys from Lecouture and took over trenches from the Inniskilling Fusiliers, these trenches were a few hundred yards more to the right than those held on the 10th May.

"A" Coy. took over the fire trench with two platoons and had two platoons in support in breastworks in front of the Rue du Bois. "C" Coy were in support of them in the breastworks behind the Rue du Bois. "B" and "C" Coys were in billets some way back on the Richebourg St. Vaast road. Our Headquarters in a house a few hundred yards behind the Rue du Bois was the most noisy place imaginable, our guns, some of which seemed to be behind every bush in the neighbourhood, kept up an intermittent and fairly heavy bombardment all night and hardly ceased for a moment until after dark the next evening.

14th. Our incessant artillery bombardment stirred up the enemy a good deal and they shelled our front trenches heavily all day with Black Marias besides heavy and light shrapnel. They also shelled the houses and breastworks

both in the front

Copy of 1/60th diary.

1915.
May 14th. (contd).. both in the front line and behind afforded very little cover from shell fire. We had one man killed and 11 wounded all by shell fire, this included 2nd Lieut.Taylor who got a small piece of shrapnel in the back of the shoulder while standing in the front trench.

Copy of 1/60th diary. (contd).

1915.
May 15th.
Heavy artillery bombardment on both sides all day. Germans especially shelled our front trenches and the Rue du Bois. We unfortunately had 3 signallers wounded during the day, one (Hunt) by a shell which burst right on their dugout in our support trenches and two (Riflemen Richards and Rifleman Seager) while up in our front trenches while reconnoitring a place to lay a wire from our front trenches forward after dark. During the morning, 2nd Lieut Fisher got a nasty wound on the back of the head. He luckily had his anti-gas mask inside the back of his cap, this formed a cushion between his head and the metal plate and tube (part of a buze) which struck him on the back of the cap. The assault on the enemy's trenches which had several times been postponed was ordered to take place at 11.30 p.m. and all final arrangements for it were made during the afternoon. The plan was roughtly as follows:

The 6th & 5th Brigades with part of the Indian Division on their left were to make a night attack on the enemy's breastworks in the neighbourhood of the Ferme du Bois.

The 6ht Brigade were on the right and the 5th on the left with the Indians beyond the latter's left flank.

The Berks and ourselves were detailed to carry out the assault which was to take place at 11.30 p.m. (Berks on right and Rifles on left) 7th Liverpools to co-operate on right of Berks. Our orders were to seize and hold the first two lines of enemy's trenches, blocking any communication trenches leading to the enemy's rear and that of the assault was successful fresh troops would be sent through those that had carried out the assault to carry on the attack about daylight.

The Battalion's 1st objective was the front line of German trenches from R2 (the left of the Berks exculsive to a bend in the enemy's breastwork (between R2 and V1)) almost opposite the Ferme du Bois. The Germans were know to have one communication trench connecting their first and second lines in this piece of their defences and also their main communication trench running past the western side of the Ferme du Bois led into their section. Their second line apparently came to a dead end about opposite our left but continued again further to the left in front of the 5th Brigade.

The German front line formed a very distinct salient from the bend mentioned as the left of our objective and several enemy's Machine Guns were known to be placed on this salient so as to be able to enfilade any attack further west. The salient was given as their objective to the right battalion of the 5th Brigade who happened to be the Inniskilling Fusiliers.

The distance from our front line to the German's was roughtly 350 yards but to our left opposite the salient this was considerably less. The ground between the opposing lines was flat mostly plough but with a good deal of r rough grass growing on it the furrows as it happened giving a very good guide for direction in the dark. There was a ditch about 12 feet wide running along parallel to and about 20 yards in front of our own front line which it however crossed near the right of our position continuing behind it.

There was also just on the enemy's side of this wide ditch an old disused trench running right along our front but this presented no serious obstacle to an advance
although it

Copy of 1/60th diary.

1915.
May 15th. (contd)

although it was very wet in places.

"D" & "B" Coys were selected to forom the two first lines "D" on right anf "B" on left, each Coy having 2 platoon in the first line and two in the second. "C" Coy was to form our third line and "A" our fourth, The Machine gun section being kept in reserve to await orders. Two two leading lines were to file out quietly by two prepared opening in our parapet and line down in front of the wide ditch ready to assault when ordered.

The left party were to cross the broad ditch by bridges which had been previous laid while the right party's opening was in front of it being just to the right xx of where this ditch entered our lines. The Battalion left its billets about 9 p.m. and everything went smoothly. Ordinary sniping (into the air) was carried on from our trenches to disarm suspicion and our artillery which had been cutting the enemysw wire by deliberate fire for several days fired an occasional,shell throughout the evening. There was no moon and the night was pretty dark. Our leading Coys filed out in silence and lay down without arousing suspicion on the enemy's sidet that anything unusual was occurring. Three signallers accompanied "D" Coy. taking with them a telephone instrument, two motor lamps, paying out telephone wire as they went. They were ordered to light one motor laps if we captured the German 1st line and two if we captured the second and were also told to signal back if other signals failed, with an electric torch by means of the Morse Code.

In our front trench we had a small dugout connected to telephone with the 6th Brigade Headquarters in a house on the Rue du Bois. The Battalion Headquarters remained close to the telephone dugout also the Machine gun section which had orders to be ready to move up but not to do so until ordered. I watched the assault from near the telephone dugout but of course owing to the darkness it was difficult to see much. For fully five minutes from 11. 30 p.m. the hour for the advance to begin nothing was visible, the Germans fired no lights and there was nothing more than the usual sniping. Then a burst of fire broken out mostly on our left and the enemy began to send up lights in all directions. One could then see silhouetted against the lights our front line which appeared to be quite close to the German trench. The whole space between the lines was dotted with men, some lying on the ground but the majority still advancing. As our front line reached the German trenches the lights from that part ceased to go up but it was possible to get glimpses of what was going on when the enemy fired lights further to our right or behind their front line. All this time a very heavy Machine Gun fire had been coming across from the salient on our left and sweeping our fronte and this fire did not seem to diminish much as time went on, rifle fire also continued from this direction. To our front there was not much fire and we anxiously awaited some signal as to what had happened. At last about 12 midnight an electric torch was visible giving a series of flashes. At first merely a succession of dots as if worked by someone who could not send Morse. Presently however KRB was sent on the torch and we knew we had secured the enemy's second line (this was a prearranged signal). A few mins later a steady light obviously one of our motor lamps was put up.

I had just finished writing out and having telephoned

to the

Copy of 1/60th diary.

1915.
May 15th.
(contd)

to the Brigade a message to tell them the situation when I noticed that the C.O had disappeared, he had arranged to let me know when he wanted the Headquarters moved over to the German lines and also presumably would give some orders for the Machine Gun Section. I received several messages from the 6th Brigade on the telephone saying that the Berks had got in and also the 5th Brigade on our left.

A good many wounded men were now beginning to come in, and Lt. J.S.Alston came back with a badly broken arm.

As no message came from the signallers who had gone out with the telephone instrument and we had no more wire I telephone to the Brigade for another reel as otherwise if we moved the Headquarters we should be out of touch with the Brigade.

I was beginning to get uneasy as to what had happened to the C.O but concluded that he must have gone over to the German trenches himself and forgotten to give men any orders or to give any to the Machine Gun Section. I asked everyone I could see if they knew where the C.O. was but no one knew, but I was told that when "C" Xoy. were starting across the open he was with them encouraging them. "C" Coy had gone some time ago and had been followed by "A". Willan however had remained in our breastwork for the time being and I consulted with him as to what it would be best to do in the absence of orders.

We decided to go across to the German trenches ourselves with the Headquarters and the Machine Gun Section as soon as our reel of wire arrived from the Brigade.

About this time Capt Bonham Carter came back from the German trenches and told us that apparently the salient on our left had not been taken as a heavy fire was coming from that direction into the back of our men. I telephoned this information down to the Brigade and Bonham Carter went off also there to make a personal report.

It now being past 2 a.m. and our reel of wire having turned up Willan, Slater and his Machine Gun Section and I with the Battalion Headquarters and the telephone started off for the captured trenches. There was a fairly heavy fire sweeping the ground from our left but we lay down whenever a light went up and got across allright except one of Machine Gun Section . On arrival at the 1st line of captured breastworks we saw that the wire in front of it had been almost completely destroyed and the breastworks themselves much damaged though not destroyed by shell fire. There were crowds of men 5 or 6 deep, Berks, Staffs, Inniskilling and Rifles all jumbled together sitting, standing or lying on our side of the breastwork and no one appeared to be making any attempt to sort them out or re-organize, which could easily have been done as there was practically no fire directed on this point. There was bombing and shooting going on some little distance to the left so Willan and I leaving the Headquarters and Machine Gun where they were moved along to the left to investigate. We got as far as where a communication trench runs back from the front line and a little further to the left there was vigorous bombing going on and the men in that part of the line were inclined to edge down our way. Willan then tried to get a Machine Gun into position to fire along the breastwork to the left and I was just collecting a few men to lie down and dig themselves in facing left to keep off some Germans who, as far as I could make out, were working along the trench from left

to right

Copy of 1/60th diary.

1915.
May 15th.
(contd)

to right, when I was hit in the thigh by a bullet apparently fired by one of these Germans. It knocked me over and I could not move for a minute or two, but after a few moments I could get along with help so shouted to my servant who was close by and with his help started off for our own lines as it was just getting light.

A few men had just started to dig a communication trench back from the captured breastwork but had only done a few yards of it, and were under a pretty heavy fire. I believe these belonged to the 5th Liverpools who had been ordered to find two Coys for the digging.

We got across all right and into our own lines which were now held by the Staffords less one Coy (Gunners) which had been sent on under orders of the Brigade to support us.

It was very slow work getting along the trench as besides its garrison it was packed with wounded. I got dressed by our stretcher bearers and then tried to make my way out by the communication trench; it was, however, for the moment impossible to do this as it was now daylight and the enemy were plastering the communication trench with high explosive shrapnel and whizz-bangs - they were also giving our front trench a very should shelling with every sort of gun. I managed to make my way down by short stages to the Oxford's dressing station on the Rue du Bois. It was very difficult to move down the communication trench which was damaged shelling and was blocked with dead and wounded. From the Oxford's dressing station I was taken down by our own stretcher bearers to our dressing station. This was very slow work owing to the very heavy shelling, we had to take cover behind one house for about 2 hours but the house got too hot and we moved on eventually arriving at the dressing station about noon. Bandsman Trotman killed while fetching a stretcher.

Casualties: 16.5.15.

Officers.

Major G.C.Shakerley, D.S.O.	Killed.
Capt. Adjt. W.S.Knox Gore, D.S.O.	Wounded.
Capt. Hon. J. Bigge.	Missing.
Capt. A.L.Bonham Carter.	Wounded.
Capt. E.A.Pauley.	Wounded.
Lieut. J.S.Alston.	Wounded.
Capt. Pardoe.	Wounded.
Lieut. W.H.Grenville-Grey.	Killed.
Lieut. A.E.Messer.	Wounded.
2nd Lieut. A.E.Dent.	Wounded.
2nd Lieut. J.S.H.James.	Killed.
Lieut. R.A.Banon.	Wounded.
2nd Lieut. C.E.Hardy.	Wounded.
2nd Lieut. C.M.Cassidy.	Killed.

Major Armytage's account.

Copy of 1/60th diary.

1915.
May 15th.
Major Armytage's -
account (contd)

Two platoons of "D" Coy. made good the 1st captured trench with the assistance of some of the Staffords and 1st King's Regt. and got in touch with 5th Brigade on their left.

Captain Willan then came up to the 2nd captured line and reported to me.

I instructed him to take command of 1st captured position and keep communication with 6th Brigade.

Captain Bonham Carter went back from 2nd captured line to report progress and was eventually wounded.

The following Officers of storming party reached the 2nd German trench:-
Major G.A.Armytage
Captain A.L.Bonham Carter (wounded later)
2nd Lieut.A.E.Dent (wounded leg and hand early in advance).
Lieut A.E.Messer (wounded hand but remained with his platoon until relieved by S.Staffs).
Lieut W.H.Grenville Grey (died of wounds).
Lieut. Wigan.
2nd Lieut K.J.B.Addy, "C" Coy and 2nd Lieut L.E.Hall "A" Coy, came up with supporting platoons. 2nd Lieut. R.H.Slater brought up 3 Machine Guns at once and the 4th during the night. During the advance 2nd Lieut J.S.H. James was killed and 2nd Lieut. C.M.Cassidy, mortally wounded.

Captain the Hon. J.N.Bigge, Captain and Adjutant W.A.C.Saunders Knox Gore, D.S.O., Captain E.A.Pauley, Lieut.J.S.Alston, and 2nd Lieut.C.E.Hardy were all wounded and a large number of senior N.C.O's

Total casualties.

	Killed.	Wounded.	Missing.	Total.
Officers	4.	9.		
Other ranks.	22.	184.	88.	= 307.

16th.
The Battalion held the captured German Trenches all day until relieved about 2 a.m., 17th by S.Staffords.
The shelling was very heavy all day, but mostly on our old first line trenches and the Rue du Bois.

17th.
On being relieved by S.Staffs. the Battalion moved into reserve trenches.

Relieved by Sirhind Brigade and moved into old billets in Richebourg St.Vaast. Very noisy as 16th Battery was just outside our Headquarters.

Casualties:- 2 Killed, 23 Wounded, 4 Missing.

18th.

Copy of 1/60th diary.

1915.
May 15th.   Battalion took part in attack on German trenches.
Reference map Festubert 1:10000.

Major Armytage's account.

1st Objective. German trenches between B2. exclusive to bend in enemy's trench between V1 and R6. keeping touch with Royal Berks Regt. on our right.

2nd Objective. Enemy 2nd Trench R5 to R7 exclusive.
At 11 p.m. the 2 storming Coys. "B" Capt. A.L.Bonham Carter, "D" Lieut. J.S.Alston under command of Major G.A.Armytage formed up as per diagram just S. of old trench S. of "A" line.

"B" Coy.
Captain E.A.Pauley.

"D" Coy.

8 Platoon.	5 Platoon.		16 Platoon.	15 Platoon.
Sgt.Hayes.	Lt. Messer.		2nd Lieut Cassidy.	Lieutenant Grenville-Grey.
Captain, A.L.Bonham Carter.		Major G.A.Armytage.	Lieutenant J.S.Alston.	
7 Platoon.	6 Platoon.		13 Platoon.	14 Platoon.
Sgt.Egginton.	2nd Lieut. James.		Sgt.Keevill.	Lieut.Wigan.

At 11.30 p.m. the first line advanced in quick time followed at a distance of 40 paces by the 2nd line.
The 3rd line "C" Coy. 'Capt. Hon.J.N.Bigge' deployed as soon as storming Coys. started.

12 Platoon.	11 Platoon.	18 Platoon.	9 Platoon.
2nd Lt.Hardy.	C/S.Wickham.	2/Lt.Addy.	2nd Lt. Dent

followed by "A" Coy - Capt F.G.Willan.

1 & 2 Platoons   3 and 4 Platoons.
                   2nd Lieut. Hall.
C.S.M.Hopkins.

The 1st line were ordered to take 1st German Trench and if successful to push on with 2nd line to 2nd German trench.
This was done without serious opposition and both lines pushed on and captured 2nd German Trench.
On reaching the 2nd German Trench some opposition was met with but the enemy bolted with the exception of some who hid in dug-outs and were quickly accounted for.
Parties worked up to right and left and communication trench was barricaded. Posts were established about 50 yards S of German Trench and parapets repaired as much as possible and touch established with Berks Regt.
The capture of 2nd line was signalled back on an Orilux lamp by pre-arranged signal K.R.B. which was duly acknowledged. "C" and "A" Coys. followed on and supported the storming Coys.
The Commanding Officer (Major G.C.Shakerley,D.S.O) accompanied "C" Coy and was mortally wounded during the advance.

Two platoons.

Copy of 1/60th diary. (contd).

1915.
May 18th.   Rested - ready to support 1st King's if required.
             Casualties - 2 wounded.
             Lieut. Grenville Grey buried at Richebourg St.Vaast.

19th.   Battalion moved to Vendin les Bethune arriving about
             9 p.m.
             About 10 p.m. Major R.G.Jelf, D.S.O. arrived from
             2nd Battalion and took over command of the Battalion.

20th.   Battalion moved into billets at Allouagne arriving
             about 12 noon.
             Lovely weather.

21st.   Coys cleaned up and refitted.
             Billeting area thoroughly cleaned.
             Lovely weather.

22nd.   General Horne, Commanding 2nd Division inspected the
             Battalion at 11.30 a.m. and complimented the Battalion
             on their excellent work on the night of 15th/16th May.
             A platoon from "B" Coy. made a new firing point on
             range originally made by 2nd Battalion.
             Very hot day.

23rd.   Headquarters and "A" Coy. attended Church parade,
             "B", "C" and "D" Coys. went to Marles les Mines for baths.
             Very hot day.
             H.R.H. the Prince of Wales came to tea.

24th.   "A" Coy. went to Marles les Mines for baths.
             Coys worked under O.C. Coys.
             "D" fax and "A" Coys. fired grouping practice on
             the range. Very hot day.

25th.   Very hot day.
             "B" and "C" Coys grouping practice on range "A" and "D"
             under O.C. Coys. training.

26th.   Very hot day.
             "A" and "D" Coys on range.
             "C" and "B" Coys training under O.C.Coys.
             The following Officers joined the Battalion from 6th
             Battalion:-

                  2nd Lieut.N.F.Drummond.)
                  2nd Lieut.C.T.J.Bevan.   )   "A" Coy.
                  2nd Lieut.B.H.Sumner.   "B" Coy.
                  2nd Lieut.J.E.M.Skinner.   "C" Coy.
                  2nd Lieut.G.J.Dewhurst.   "C" Coy.
                  2nd Lieut.W.C.Smith.   "D" Coy.

             Sports "A" and "D" Coys. "A" were the winners.

             10. R. transferred from 2nd Battalion.

27th.   Colder day.
             Reconnoitring party, Major Armytage and an Officer
             from each Coy. and M.G.Officer proceeded to Grenay to inspect
             French trenches to be taken over by Battalion.
             Coys. under O.C. Coys.

                                                            28th.

Copy of 1/60th diary (contd).

1915.
May 28th.   Standing by to move to trenches.
            Move cancelled, Coys. under O.C.Coys.
            Machine Gunners on range in afternoon.

29th.   Fine day. Coys. on range and under their O.C, for training.
            1 Officer (2nd Lieut. Heyrick, "B" Co.) and 93 other ranks joined Battalion.

30th.   Sunday - Church Parade. The Bishop of Khartoum took the service and preached a very good sermon.
            After the service the G.O.C.6th Brigade bade farewell to the Brigade on taking over Command of South Midland 47th Territorial Division. He was very complimentary about the work the Battalion had done during his period of Command of the Brigade.
            At 1.45 p.m. the Brigade marched to Grenay to take over trenches from the French Army halting en route at Houchin for 2 hours and relieving the 239th Battalion of the 58th Corps in sub-section W.I.
            The order of march was "B", "A", "C", "D".
            "B" and "A" Coys took over the front line, "C" in close support in second line, and "D" in reserve.
            Headquarters in a house in the village
            Relief completed at 1 a.m.
            Very quiet night.
            Trenches good and left beautifully clean.
            4 Machine Guns in firing line.
            Brigadier General A.C.Daly took over command of the Brigade on arrival at Les Brebis. 3 officers, 2nd Lieut.E.M.Allfrey ("A" Coy), 2nd Lieut. R.S.H.Stafford ("C" Coy), and 2nd Lieut. M.T.Sampson ("D" Coy) joined the Battalion during the march at Moeux les Mines.

31st.   Fine day and quiet.
            The Germans put some heavy shells into Grenay but only wounded about 6 people, 3 being civilians.
            French Artillery only in support of our line.
            The G.O.C 6th Brigade visited Battalion Headquarters in the afternoon.
            Casualties- 1 man wounded.

COPY.

6th Infantry Brigade.
2nd Division.

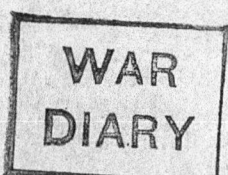

1st BATTN. THE KING'S ROYAL RIFLE CORPS

J U N E

1 9 1 5

Copy.   1st Battn. The King's Royal Rifle Corps.

Diary 1/60th. June 1915,

1st.   G.O.C.s, 2nd Div., 6th Bde, and 4th Bde visited trenches at 7.30
        a.m. Fairly quiet day. Enemy put several "pip-squeaks" over
        abt noon owing to a party of another regt. washing in full
        view- result we had 1 K, and 4 W. Later 3 more men were W.

2nd.   Quiet day. Were relvd abt 9.30p.m. By R.Berks. Moved into
        Billets at Les Brebis. Men b'lltd in Miners houses. Relf
        completed abt 2a.m. 3rd June.

3rd.   Rested. As no movement was allowed during daylight arrgts
        were made for men to have baths at Mines. The following
        telegram was sent to His Majesty on the occasion of his
        b'day:-
        " Equerry, Buckingham Palace, London. " All ranks 1st Bn,
        60th Rifles, beg humbly to offer their congratulations on his
        Majesty's birthday.
                                        Commanding."

        The following were awarded the D.C.M. 4050 Sgt. Robinson. J.
        6239 Actg.Sgt Crooks. W. 7338 L/c McCullah.C.

4th.   Rested all day. Bn had baths in the Mine. Recvd following
        wire from His Majesty in reply to ours of y'day:-
        " Officer Commanding, 1st Bn 60th Rifles, 6th I.Bde. Exp.Force.
        " I have recvd with much pleasure the message contained in
        yr telegram, will you convey my sincerer thanks to all rks
        for their congratulations and good wishes. George R.I. Col.-
        in-Chief. "

5th.   Rested all day. 68 o.r. jnd.

6th.   Chucrch Parade at 10a.m. In the evg the Bde were relvd by
        the 141st Bde at 11p.m. The 23rd Bn Lon.Regt., relvd us at
        12 m.n. The Bn mrchd at 1a.m. to billets at Noeux les Mines
        arrvg at 2.30a.m.

7th.   Beautiful weather. 6th Bde relvd the 141st Bde in the Vermell
        -es district. The Bn took over the trenches held by the 7th
        Lond. at Routoire Farme at 11p.m. Relief complete by 1.30am
        on 8th inst.

8th.   Beautiful weather - Hot. Cleaned up trenches wh were v dirty
        Trenches were v well built but al chalk, and abt 800 yds from
        Ger.lines. A and B cos in f/trench;C in res. trench., D in
        sppt/t. No cas. B.Gen.Daly went round the trenches.

9th.   V quiet day. G.O.C. 2nd Div. & Bgdr. came round the line at
        8a.m. A and B cos relvd by C and D cos resp. Little shell-
        ing by "pip-squeaks". No cas.

10th.   Warm sunny day. Enemy art. rather more active and "pip-
        squeaked" our front line blowing in portions of our parapet.
        Unfort.Lt.G.T.J.Bevan was W by one of these shells. No
        other cas. During the evg. rain set in and it was a wet
        night. One Sgt.McKiddie went to visit a list.post. and dis-
        appeared. It is thought that he must have been caught by a
        Ger. patrol.

11th.   Trenches in a v sticky condtn owing to wet last night. The
        day being somewhat cloudy, enemy art. quieter than y'day. The
        Bn was relvd by 1st King's at 10.30pm. On relief being com-
        pleted at m.n. the Coys mrchd independently to billets at
        La Bourse. No cas.

                                                              12th.

Copy.

Diary of 1/60th, June 1915. (contd).

12th.   Bn arrvd into billets at La Bourse abt 4a.m. Most of the day was spent in cleaning up billets wh were left in a shock-ing state and also cleaning equipt. wh was v chalky from the trenches.

13th.   Ch.Par. at La Bourse, at wh G.O.C. 2nd Div., who was present congratulated the men who had recently won the D.C.M. in the Bde. R/men Miles and Hyles of the Bn were amongst the awards

14th.   Lovely day.

15th.   V hot day. Cos. training under O.C.Cos. in the mng. In the a'noon the Bde was relvd by the 5th Bde and the R.Inn.took over our billets, the Bn moving at 5p.m. to La Pugnoy raking over billets from H.L.I. Bn arrvd at La P. at 8p.m. Billets v fair and clean. Maj.Jelf apptd tempy. Lt.Col.

16th.   Lovely weather. Bn carried out Co training under O.C.Cos. B coy went to range at Allouagne. C co went to range at Bois-des-Dames.

17th.   The weather was v fine and hot. Bn in Corps Res. and under 2 hrs notice to move. This was cancelled in the a'noon.

18th.   Fine day and v hot. Coys carried out training under O.C.cos A co went to Marles les Mines for baths. B.Gen.Daly came round in the a'noon. In the Lon.Gaz. the following were mentioned in despatches. Maj.Shakerley,D.S.O.,Capt.Pardoe, Capt.Bonham-Carter,Capt.Saunders-Knox-Gore,D.S.O.,Capt.E.P. Shakerley,Capt.Woods,Capt.Willan,Lt.Lloyd,Lt.Fisher,Lt.Slater Lt.Else,Lt.and Q.M.Harman, 7013 A/C.S.M.Cockayne,9980 RSM Tedder,1945 L/Cpl Higney,1486 L/Cpl Campling,4981 Rfn.Martinelli,5037 Rfn Reidy, 5036 L/Cpl Reidy,11259 Rfn.Pocock.

19th.   Cooler day but v quiet time. Coy.training was cancelled owing to orders having been recdv to move to Verquigneul. This move was carried out at 2.30p.m. Bn arrvd in new billets at Verquig: at 5.30pm.m Billets poor.

20th.   Fine weather continues. Bn spent most of day in cleaning up billets and b'lltg area. Cos. paraded under O.C.cos.

21st.   The Bde having taken over trenches from the 1st Div.on the evg of 19th at Guni Guinchy the Bn whilst in billets are divl. res.

22nd.   Cos paraded under O.C.Cos.

23rd.   Fine hot weather. Bn relvd S.Staffs in trenches S of La Bassee just S of Guni Guinchey,at 6p.m. Trenches were fairl good. V active part of the line. A and B cos and C in firing line and D in sppt. The Lon.Gaz. of this date publd. the following rewards:- Capt.F.G.Willan awarded the D.S.O. Capt. Woods the M.C., Lt.Fisher the M.C., Lt.Lloyd the M.C., Hon.Lt.& Q.Mr.Harman to be Hon.Capt. 5/4731 Rfn Hyles the D.C.M. 11755 Rfn.Miles the D.C.M. and 11935 L/Cpl the D.C.M.

24th.   Fairly quiet day. Gers. v busy in crater adjng their line. In the evg enemy Minenwerfer were rather active.

                                                                25th.

Copy.

Diary of 1/60th, June 1915 (contd). and July.

25th. Fine day. B.Gen. Daly went round the line at abt 6.30pm
Gers. v active with bombs, esp. on the lip of Vesuvius Crater
where we were building a ppst as look out to this crater wh
was occpd by night by Gers. In the eg. our miners discovered that the Gers. were mining, on top of us just N of
Vesuvius. At abt 4.pm. we therefore decided to blow up our
mine and successfully blew up theirs. The explosion being
close to our lines portion of our parapet fell in burying
some of our men temprly. During the ngt the Gers. gave us
some "Hate" with bombs, pip-squeaks, and minnies.

26th. Busy day spent in rebuilding parapets damaged by the mine
on the previous day. Also finishing off post on Vesuvius.
812 Cpl. F.L.Hyes and 4846 L/Cpl White awarded the D.C.M.
Night fairly normal, anem not so active. Capt.&Q.M. Harman
d of w recvd on the rd nr Beuvry. He was going to the asstce
of a Fr. woman wheeling a child in a perambulator during
some shelling when he was hit by shrapnel.

27th. V hot day. Bn relvd by S.Staffs. Gers. were fairly quiet all
day. Went into billets at Annequin wh were not v good.

28th. Rested and cleaned up billets, also general clean up of Bn.

29th. In billets. B co recvd instrctn from our Gren. Coy bombers.

30th. In billets. Fine weather. In a'noon enemy shelled the village one bursting in the main rd outside one of our billets
wounding 1 o.r. in the arm.

2nd Division
War Diaries
1st Battn, Kings Royal Rifles.
1st July to 17th December 1915

COPY

6th Infantry Brigade.
2nd Division.

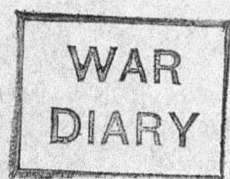

1st BATTN. THE KING'S ROYAL RIFLE CORPSY

J U L Y

1 9 1 5

1st Battn. The King's Royal Rifle Corps.

July 1915

July 1st. Relvd S.Staffs Regt, in the trenches at 3p.m. A,B and D in the firing line. C in sppt. The night was fine & passed off ~~quiet-quietly.~~ quite quietly.

The entries from the 15th June to the 1st July are "inserted" in the Diary. The entry in the Diary for the 1st July reads as follows:-
" The Bn relvd S,Staffs,in the area just S of La Bassee Road from GunSt to the Vermelles - La B rd, A.B.D. cos in front line , C in sppt. The line rather badly smashed by shelling in the mng. A good deal of ~~shelling~~ bombing during the night."

2nd. A little shelling with pip-squeaks but otherwise quiet mng. At 10p.m. Gers. started rapid fire and hvy bombing wh lasted for abt an hr - nothing developed from so concluded it to be "wind-up." Rest of day and night fairly quiet. 2nd Lt. J.W.E.Paul jnd the Bn and was posted to A coy.

3rd. Germans shelled Cambrin somewhat hvily also put some pip-squeaks over our front line.

4th. Quite a quiet day only a little usual bombing. The ngt was the quietest night we have had there up to date.

5th. Quiet mng - relvd by 2nd C.G.at 2.30pm - marched to billets in Bethune, arrvg there abt 6.30pm. The billets were quite good and clean.

6th. Bn rested and cleaned up. Gers.shelled an obsvn.balloon wh was nr the town, a few shell dropping nr the stn. V stromy night, hvy rain and wind.

7th. Resting. The cos at disposal of their O.C.s

8th. Bn lined the rd for Ld.Kitchener.

9th.

Copy.

Diary of 1/60th, July 1915.

9th.   Bn still in billets. Cps. paraded under O.C.Cos.

10th.   In Bethune - Cos. paraded under O.C.Cos. Bn gave a concert in the theatre in the evg. 43 o.r. jnd.

11th.   In Bethune. Ch.Parade.

12th.   "   Cos paraded under O.C.cos.

13th.   The Bde moved up into the line, taking over the Givenchy sect. from 5th Bde. The Bn went into new billets at Le Quesnoy.

14th.   Quiet day but the bn had to find w.ps all day and night for R.E. in the firing line. Either carrying parties for R.E. or pumping fatigues for the Mining coy.

15th.   Bn found w.ps all the day and night for R.E. same as y'day.

16th.   The Bn relvd the Berks at Givenchy taking over the line from the Fr. Farm on our R to the Willows. A and C in the firing line, A on R C on L, B in close sppt and D at Windy corner in billets. A lot of work needed on trenches to make parapets bullett proof and also to heighten them. At 11pm Gers. opened a burst of rapid fire in front of A coy and followed up by some shelling with hvy shells on Scottish Trench, v little damage and did not last more than half an hr.

17th.   Quiet day. Gers. shelled nr B.H.Q. and D coy abt lucnh time but did no damage. V quiet night.

18th.   B and D cos relvd A and C resp. in a'noon. The day was quiet but a little hate at night.

19th.   Fairly quiet day. D coy were shelled a bit in the mng no damage being done. In the evg Gers. shelled out btties in the woods abt a mile S of Bn H.Q. v hvily with 6" mostly.

20th.   Qt.mng. The Bn was relvd by Berks at abt 3p.m. & went back into billets at Le Quesnoy.

21st.   Pumping fatigues for miners and R.E. carrying parties, continuously day and night every 4 hrs. Capt.SH.Ferrand from 3rd bn jnd and took over C coy. A draft of 54 NCOs and men came with Capt.Ferrand.

22nd.   w.ps and fatigues all day. Gers. shelled Beauvry and drop some shells among Indian R.G.A. mules in wood just behind Bn.H.Q. killing 2 or three but doing no damage to us. 2nd Lt.E.H.Fangwell from 6th Bn jnd and was posted to D coy.

23rd.   w.ps and fatigues continuos all day as usual - otherwise qt. day. 2nd Lt.Belchambe jnd and was posted to A coy.

25th.   The bn relvd the Berks in trenches 7am. Fairly qt mng. Abt 2.30pm the Gers. suddenly opened t.m fire on C co in Scott Scottish Trench, one burst on the parapet just off Gallow Gate & W 2nd Lt Dewhurst rahter badly in shoulder. Capt.E.B.Denison rejnd Bn. A and C cos in firing line, D in sppt, and B at Windy Corner.

                                                                26th.

Copy.

Diary of 1/60th, July 1915.(contd).

26th. Mng and a'noon was qt. At 6pm the Gers. blew up a mine in front of A coy wh did no damage to us, it made a small crater abt 30 yds from our front line. The Gers. followed the mine with bombs and quite a lot of bombs t.ms and a little shelling but no cas. resulted from this. A co worked hard that night cutting a trench from our line to the crater, this was partially completed by the mng. It was sufficient to enable us to enter the crater and estb a post on the E lip of it wh we were able to hold during the next day.

27th. Gers. shelled the sppt trenches New Cut and Park Lane during the mng. D and B relvd C and A cos in the front line. A & B contd. work on the new crater wh is to be called in future Riflemen's Crater. The post on the E lip was strengthened and a traverse was built also a trench was started wh was to go all the way round inside the crater. This work was contd. all day and all the night with a party of R.E. to hel in s'bagging the post and E lip.

28th. Fairlt qt. day. Work on Riflemen's Crater contd. Very good headway made during night,. At 6pm the Gers. blew up another mine abt 50 yds from B cos front line and abt 40 yds S.E. of R'men's Crater. It did no damage to our trench but a few men were hit by splinters and lumps of earth.
The Bgdr. was v anxious for us to try and occpy the new Crater. The Col. decided to send out a recnntrg. party wh Capt.Willan, A coy, did, and it was reptd by this patrol that the Gers. had gained possession of the nr(E) lip but that the (W) lip(nearest to us was unoccpd. Col. Jelf decided that A and B shd sap out to within ten yds of the New crater, (bombing distance) and to continue the sap to within 10 yds (bombing distance if necessary) of R'men's Crater, and back to our front line. A coy sent out a covering party under 2nd Lt.Goodwin and some bombers to lie on the W lip of this New Crater and keep the Gers. heads down by bombing them occasionally. Abt 9pm just after the w.ps had started digging the Germans opened rapid fire and sent over 3 t.ms together and some pip-squeaks; this lasted abt 20 mins. It rather stopped the w.ps for a time but we only had 4 or 5 cas. and these were slight ones. As soon as it was all qt. again the w.ps started once more and worked steadily all the night. They completed the trench almost all the way thro enough to est. a bombing post abt 10 yds from this New Crater All thro the spell of rapid fire etc. the covering party on the lip with 2nd Lt.Goodwin remnd there and did good work.

29th. Early mng quite qt, but at abt 8a.m. Gers. shelled sppt line and around Herts redoubt continuously for ¾ hr with hvies fortunately doing no damage. Rest of day qt. At 5pm the Gds. Bde. relvd the 6th Bde the I.G.s relvg this Bn. On relief the Bn.marched to billets at Essars wh were v poor and far from clean, and men were v crowded.

30th. Rested and Bn cleaned up & washed. 2nd Lt.V.N.E.Howard Vincent jnd and was posted to C Coy.

31st. Bn had the swimming baths at Bethune from 8 till 10a.m. Coys bathed every ½ hr.

1/60th 6th B.n

1915
July 29th the Guards Brigade relieved the 6th Brigade the Irish
(contd.) Guards relieving this Battalion. On relief the Battalion
marched to billets at Essars which were very poor and far
from clean, and men were very crowded.

30th Rested, and Battalion cleaned up and washed.
2nd Lieut. V.H.E.Howard-Vincent joined and was posted to
"C" Coy.

31st Battalion had the swimming-baths at Bethune from
8 till 10 a.m. Coys. bathed every half hour.

6th Infantry Brigade.
2nd Division.

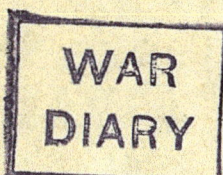

1st BATTN. THE KING'S ROYAL RIFLE CORPS.

A U G U S T

1 9 1 5

1st Battalion The King's Royal Rifle Corps.

August 1915

Augt. 1st   Quiet day. Church Parade in the morning.

2nd   In Essars. Coys. at the disposal of their Os.C.

3rd   Battalion moved at 5 a.m. to take over fresh billets from 5th and 7th King's Liverpools at Vendin, relief completed by 8 a.m. In the afternoon the Brigade held a Horse Show at the Bethune Sports Ground.

4th   Companies paraded under O.C.Coys. in the morning "C" Coy. doing bombing under Brigade Bombers.

5th   Companies paraded under O.C.Coys. In the afternoon Battalion marched to Beuvry and inspected our second line there. Companies marched back independently to Vendin. Lieut and Qr Master W. BECK joined the Battalion on promotion.

1915.
Augt. 6th   Companies paraded under O.C Coys. in the morning.
               Rest of day quiet.

       7th   The Brigade took over the line from La Bassee Road
               to Canal. The Battalion going into line from the La Bassee
               Road to Ridley Walk. Only 2 Platoons and a half front,
               "B" Coy. in front line at Oxford Street, "C" Coy. 1
               Platoon Stafford Redoubt, and 3 Platoons Cambrin Support
               Point, "D" Coy. 2 Platoons Harley Street and 1 Platoon
               Praed Street and 1 in Marylebone Road. "A" Coy. in
               billets (cellars) at Toubieres. Quiet night.

       8th   Quiet day, occasional shelling with "pip-squeaks"
               especially at 6 p.m. About 11.30 p.m. we had a wiring
               party out from "D" Coy. under 2nd Lieut. Sampson with a
               covering party from "B" out in front. Shortly after this
               the Germans who had evidently spotted this party suddenly
               opened rapid fire on it and also trench mortars and a
               few "pip-squeaks". The wiring party managed to get in
               quite safely but 2 men of the covering party were killed
               and a third wounded. This put a stop to any further
               wiring that night. Remainder of the night was quiet.

       9th   Quiet day, occasionally worried by Minenwerfers but
               our guns replied at once by sending over 2 shells to one
               Minnie. Night quiet.
               Lieut A.J. Austen-Cartmell rejoined the Bn and took over command of B Coy.

1915
Augt. 10th   Quiet morning, a few "pip-squeaks" after lunch no
damage done. "C" Coy. relieved "B" in front line "B" Coy.
moves back to Toubieres and "A" Coy. moves up to Cambrin
Support Point. The 2nd Battalion holding the front line
on our right and adjoining us. Quiet night.

11th   Germans shelled our trenches all the morning, but
fortunately either just on our left or our right and
therefore did no damage. The night was as usual fairly
quiet.

12th   The day was moderately quiet but for an occasional
Minnie and a few "pip-squeaks", about 10 p.m. the Germans
had "wind up" and started bombing followed by rather
heavy trench mortar fire which lasted for some time but
no damage was done.

13th   Germans very active with Rifle Grenades and we are
unable to reply as Rifle Grenades are impossible to
obtain. 5th King's Liverpools relieved half of our
Battalion and took over the front line from "C" Coy.
Battalion Headquarters "C" and "A" Coy. move back to
billets in Beuvry "D" Coy. at Cambrin Support Point and
"B" Coy. at Toubieres who are under the Command of the
Colonel Commanding 5th King's Liverpools.

1915
Augt. 14th   "A" and "C" Coys. had to find large working parties
of 250 men all the morning for R.E. at Cambrin and
Pont Fixe. 1.O.R joined

15th   Same working parties from "A" and "C" as yesterday.
2 O.R joined

16th   Same working parties in the morning. In the
afternoon "A" and "C" Coys. relieved "D" and "B" Coys.
respectively at Cambrin Support Point and Toubieres
"D" and "B" Coys. returning to billets at Beuvry.

17th   Same working parties found by "B" and "D" Coy. all
the morning for R.E.

18th   No working parties as the Battalion returns to the
trenches.
    Battalion relieves 5th King's Liverpools in the
trenches at 3 p.m. "D" Coy. in front line. "B" Coy.
2 Platoons Harley Street, 1 Platoon Praed Street, 1 Platoon
Marylebone Road. Quite a quiet night.

19th   Quiet day. A little shelling but no damage done.
Night was also quiet.

20th   Very quiet day, one or two Minnies were fired but
dropped in the Brick Stacks. The night was also peaceful.
8 O.R joined

1915
Aug. 21st   In the afternoon "A" Coy. relieved "D" Coy. in the
front line, "D" Coy. going back to Toubieres and "C" Coy.
going to Harley Street and "B" Coy. to Cambrin. Germans
were rather active with Rifle Grenade during the day and
also at night.

1 Other rank joined

22nd   Germans very active with Rifle Grenades and "pip-
squeaks" most of the day. At night about 9 p.m. the
Germans started some hate and sent over Rifle Grenades 3
at a time in Waterloo Place, our extreme right. "A" Coy.
had bad luck having one Sergeant (Penn) and 3 L./Cpls.
and a Rifleman hit (the Rifleman being killed) all with
Rifle Grenades. After 10.30 p.m. all was quiet.

23rd   "B" Coy. relieved "A" Coy. in front line, "A" Coy.
going back to Toubieres. Brigadier of 19th Brigade visited
the trenches as his Brigade was to relieve us next day.
The day was quiet as our guns had retaliated well the
previous night. The night also was fairly quiet.

50 OR joined

24th   The Battalion was relieved by 1st Cameron Highlanders
at 3 p.m. Relief completed by 5 p.m. when the battalion
marched into billets at Bethune.

25th   In Bethune. Resting.

*London Gazette 25/8/15. Decorations conferred by
H.I.M. The Emperor of Russia —
4050 Sgt Robinson   Cross of the order of St George 4th Class
1486 " Campling   Medal of St George 4th Class
11259 L/C Pocock   "   "   "   "*

```
1915
Augt.26th         In Bethune.    Resting.

     27th         In Bethune.    Resting.

     28th         The Battalion paraded to march off at 12.30 p.m. as
                  the Brigade were moving back to fresh billets W. of
                  Lillers. The Battalion marched to Norrent Fontes where
                  the billets were respectable arriving there about 6.30 p.m.
                  having had teas on the way.
                           H O R Jones
     29th         Norrent Fontes.    Field Training.

     30th         Norrent Fontes.    Field Training.

Augt.31st         Norrent Fontes.    Field Training.
```

6th Infantry Brigade.
2nd Division.

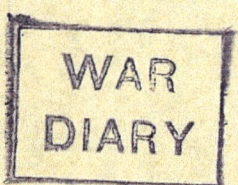

1st BATTN. THE KING'S ROYAL RIFLE CORPS.

S E P T E M B E R

1 9 1 5

1st Battalion The King's Royal Rifle Corps.

September 1915

Sept. 1st   Norrent Fontes.   Field Training.
            Capt F.G.Willan D.S.O. promoted Major

2nd   Norrent Fontes.   Field Training.

3rd   Brigade moved to Gonnehem the Battalion leaving at
            2 p.m. very unpleasant march as it rained hard all the
            way and found very poor billets on arrival there,
            fortunately it was only for one night.

4th   Battalion moved off at 10.30 a.m. and halted at
            Vendin at 12 noon for dinners moving off again at 1.30 p.m.
            for Cambrin to take over the line from S.of La Bassee Road

104.

1915
Sept. 4th
(Contd.)   to the Vermelles – La Bassee Road. "C" Coy. on the right, "B" Coy. in centre, "D" Coy. on the left, "A" Coy. in support. Trenches in a perfectly filthy condition. The night was fairly quiet but cold.

2/Lt O.R. Joiner

5th   Fairly quiet. A certain amount of bombing. "C" Coy. had one man killed by sniper. The night was fairly quiet.

Capt Miller RAMC transferred to No 6 Fd Ambulance Capt Talbot RAMC joined

6th   Fairly quiet except for trench mortars on our left and centre Coys. doing very little damage to the trench and no casualties.

7th   German snipers very active – killing a Corporal in "C" Coy. Sniping continued most of the day and with great activity at night.

8th   The Battalion was relieved at 9.30 a.m. by the 1st Herts. and went into billets at Annequin.

9th   In Annequin, fatigues all the morning for R.E.
Major Millar appointed Bde Major 5th Infy Bde.

10th   In Annequin, more fatigues for R.E.

11th   In Annequin.

12th   The Battalion went into the trenches again relieving the 1st Herts. "C" Coy. on the right, "A" Coy. in the centre, "D" Coy. on the left, "B" Coy. in support. Quiet night. *2/Lt Belchambers left for the Base*

1915
Sept.13th   Quiet day - a little sniping and bombing but nothing more than usual. Early part of the night there was a good deal of activity by German snipers.

14th   Another quiet day bar a few Rifle Grenades. Quiet night.

15th   Germans rather more active with Rifle Grenades during the morning but our Siege Battery retaliated during the afternoon on their front line.

16th   The Battalion should have been relieved but owing to 5th King's Liverpools being withdrawn from the Brigade we had to stop another night and then be relieved by the 19th Brigade. Germans very quiet especially their guns, our guns are and have been very active lately. The night passed quite quietly.

17th   Brigade was relieved by the 19th Brigade. The A and S Highlanders relieved "A", "B" and "D" Coys. The Middlesex relieved "C" Coy. Relief completed by 5 p.m. the Battalion marching back to billets at Annequin The billets were not good.

1915
Sept.18th   Battalion cleaned up. Coys. paraded under Os-C.Coys.
In the afternoon rehearsed the whole Battalion for
carrying up the accessory which they had to do at night.
The whole Battalion was on this fatigue. There were
148 jackets to be carried up requiring 666 N.C.O's and
Riflemen and 9 Officers. The Battalion paraded at
6.45 p.m. at Hedgerow Lane there were 9 detachments in
all — 8 detachments consisting of 16 jackets with 4 men
to each jacket — 4 jackets made a group and there were
2 N.C.O's to each group, the 9th detachment was 20 jackets.
The 1st detachment left at 9 p.m. and the last at 11.30 p.m

19th   Quiet all day. Battalion rested. At 7.15 p.m. the
Battalion paraded for the jacket fatigue the same as the
previous evening, the number of jackets being the same —
148.

20th   The Battalion moved up from their billets at Annequin
at 5.30 p.m. to the following positions, "A" and "C" Coys.
into cellars at Pont Fixe, 2 Platoons of "D" Coy. in
Cuinchy Support Point, 2 Platoons of "D" Coy. in Cambrin
Support Point, "B" Coy. in cellars in Houses on N. side
of main La Bassee Road. Battalion Headquarters remained
at Annequin, at 7.15 p.m. 9 Officers and 296 Riflemen and

1915
Sept.20th
(Contd.)   74 N.C.O's paraded at Hedgerow Lane for carrying up 74 jackets, to 74 emplacements in the firing line.

21st   The four days bombardment started at 7 a.m. Battalion Headquarters moved up to Old Brigade Headquarters from Annequin at 6 a.m. where it remained until the evening of the 24th. Bombardment was quite mild during the day and very little hostile artillery fire indeed. Fairly quiet night not much firing. At 7.15 p.m. 9 Officers, 37 N.C.O's and 148 Riflemen paraded at Hedgerow Lane to carry up 37 jackets to the 37 emplacements in the firing line.

22nd   The weather was dull. The bombardment continued but still the enemy's guns remained very silent. One unlucky hostile shell burst in Cuinchy Support Point and wounded 4 - 2 very seriously. The day passed without further incident.

23rd   The bombardment still continues. "D" Coy. at Cambrin Support Point had 3 premature bursts in their billets one hitting the house of their Coy. Headquarters which hit 2nd Lieut.B.H.Sumner very slightly in the head. The shells or fuze caps were found in all three cases to belong to a Field Battery firing on the S. side of the

1915
Sept.23rd
(Contd.)   La Bassee Road. No further casualties occurred. There
was rather more night firing than there had been on the
two previous nights.

24th   The bombardment increased rather during the day but
still the enemy's guns were very quiet. At 5.30 p.m. the
battalion moved up into battle position. Headquarters
moved up to Woburn Abbey with "C" Coy. in Sidings off
Glasgow Road. "A" Coy. moved to Cambrin Support Point
and "D" Coy. with its 2 Platoons from Cuinchy went into
cellars adjoining "B" Coy., "B" Coy. remaining in the same
place. Advanced Brigade Headquarters were in No. 6
Siding off Glasgow Road.

25th   During the night of 24th/25th our Artillery was
very active and much heavier than it previously had been.
At midnight the Brigade informed us that the hour of
Zero for the attack would be 5.50 a.m. For one whole
hour previous to this the guns had been engaged in a very
heavy bombardment. At 5.10 a.m. 6 jackets of the accessory
were turned on but this was contrary to all wishes of the
Experts who declared that the wind was quite unfavourable.
The morning being very damp and inclined to rain and a very
variable wind from S.E. to S. and S.W. but as the order
was definitely given the accessory had to be used. The

1915
Sept. 25th
(Contd.)   Battalion being in Brigade reserve waited orders all day to move but owing to the non-success of the accessory no movement could be successful and the day passed without any orders coming as our attack had been held up. At 10 p.m. orders were received from the Brigade that the Battalion together with the 1st Royal Berkshire Regiment and 2nd Worcesters were to form a Composite Brigade under Lieut.-Colonel Carter and to move from Annequin at 7 a.m. to Vermelles.

26th   At 2 a.m. an order was received that the Battalion was to move as soon as possible. The Battalion moved at 3.15 a.m. assembling at old Brigade Headquarters then marching from Annequin to Vermelles, just before reaching Vermelles Colonel Carter met us and took Colonel Jelf with him to 7th Division Headquarters (This Composite Brigade being attached to this Division). The Battalion moved into cover of ruined Houses and billeted there at Vermelles. At 6 a.m. Colonel Jelf returned to say that he had orders to go at once and command a Brigade in the 9th Division, and that Major Armytage, who at once took command of the Battalion, was to report to Colonel Carter at 7th Division Headquarters. Major Armytage returned at 8.55 a.m. with the orders that the Battalion was to fall in at 9 a.m.

110.

1915
Sept.26th
(Contd.)

and that the Battalion with the Worcesters were to attack Citie St.Elie. The attack was ordered for 11 a.m. but we were not to move until orders were received from Colonel Carter. At 12 noon an order came cancelling this attack, but ordering the 2nd Worcesters with ½ Battalion 1/K.R.R.C. in support to attack the Quarries at 4 p.m. and that there would be one hour's bombardment before. At 1.15 p.m. the Worcesters moved up via Gordon Alley and Hulloch Alley to old German Front Line Trench in front of the Quarries. They were followed by "A" and "C" Coys under Captain E.B.Denison as support. At 4 p.m. the Worcesters attacked but their advance was too much to the left, and, in consequence, Captain Denison was ordered to push "A" Coy. up on the Worcesters right. At about 8.30 p.m. Major G.A.Armytage received orders to bring the remaining half Battalion up to the old British Front Line. Having arrived there about 11 p.m. Major Armytage moved his Headquarters forward to old German Front Line Trench where "C" Coy. were holding the line of support to "A" Coy.

The night passed without further incident everyone being busy consolidating the position.

About 10 p.m. a congratulatory wire was received through Carters Brigade from General Gough Commanding 1st Corps

1915
Sept.26th
(Contd.)

(A full account of the attack, 26th Sept.)

At 1.30 p.m. on 26th at Vermelles, "A" and "C" Coys. - Machine Guns 1st K.R.R. under Captain Denison were ordered to support the Worcesters under Colonel Lambton in an attack on the Quarries, W.of Citie St.Elie, to be preceded by a 2 hour's bombardment commencing at 2.30 p.m. The Quarries had been previously taken, but had been lost. Route from Vermelles - communication trench Gordon Alley - Hulloch Alley - Border Lane - Old English Front Line - German Trench. Owing to delay by Worcesters in communication trench the attack commenced 20 minutes late. At 4.50 p.m. the Worcesters deployed by half-companies from the German Trench between Citie St.Elie Avenue and Breslau Avenue two communication trenches S.W. of the Quarries meeting with cross machine gun and rifle fire, and advanced across the open towards the Quarries. In the meantime "C" Coy. under Captain S.H.Ferrand had arrived in the Old British Trench. "A" Coy. under 2nd Lieut.Bevan took up a position in German Trench near point 34, ready to support Worcesters At 5.20 p.m. it was reported that the Worcesters were progressing well but required re-inforcements. 2nd Lieut.Hall was ordered to advance with his Platoon and was followed by 2nd Lieut.Paul with his Platoon. It was then reported that the Quarries

1915
Sept.26th
(Contd.)

had been taken, but more re-inforcements were required. 2nd Lieut.Bevan was ordered to send up two more Platoons to the Front Line. 2nd Lieut.Bevan was wounded in the hip. "C" Coy. had been ordered to come up to the German Trench and had arrived. 2nd Lieut.K.J.B.Addy with one Platoon had orders to reinforce the right flank but lost direction and took up a position in St.Elie Avenue. 2nd Lieut.J.E.M.Skinner followed with his Platoon, but was wounded in the leg. 2nd Lieut.R.S.H.Stafford then followed with his Platoon but, owing to darkness having come on it was difficult to keep the proper direction. He was ordered to re-inforce the right flank. He arrived at German Trench running S.of point 78 and was wrongly directed by a Sergeant of the Worcesters to a N.E.direction where the Worcesters were supposed to be near point 90. He came under heavy Machine Gun and Rifle fire close to the German wire, losing 12 men, but under cover of darkness later on was able to withdraw his Platoon and carry all his wounded back to Quarry Support Trench. At 7.30 p.m. the Machine Guns under 2nd Lieut.R.H.Slater were ordered to go forward and take up suitable positions in the captured trenches. It was reported that no more re-inforcements were needed. Captain Ferrand with 2 Platoons was left in German Trench. Captain Denison went

1915
Sept.26th
(Contd.)

forward to reconnoitre and found that St.Elie Avenue was held half way with a barricade - Bombers went forward, and it was then found out that St.Elie Avenue Trench was unoccupied by the Germans as far as a cutting in the Road near point 90. 2nd Lieut.Addy was ordered to place a barricade to cover the cutting.

The situation at the Quarries was as follows:- The Worcesters had <u>not</u> taken the Quarries as was at first reported, but two German Trenches about 300 yards S.W. of the Quarries. The Worcesters held the front trench, and "A" Coy. with 5 Sections of "C" Coy. held trench running S. from point 78 with Worcesters in the right half of it. These trenches were consolidated. The support trench was barricaded S. of point 78 - point 90. The Quarries and the trench immediately S. of Quarries remained in the hands of the Germans. The supporting Platoons advanced extremely well and in good order. The other half of the Battalion came up to the German Trench about midnight under Major G.A.Armytage.

2nd/Lt R.J Bevan + Lt S Kinnear wounded

27th   The morning was quiet. At 1 p.m. an order was received that 1st K.R.R.C. and 1st R.Berks Regiment will make an attack on the Quarries this afternoon at 4 p.m. 1st Royal Berks will be on the right and advancing from

1915
Sept.27th
(Contd.)

Old German Front Line Trench will pass through 2nd Worcesters who will remain where they are at present in support.

1st K.R.R.C. will attack on the left, the half Battalion in support moving up and joining the half Battalion at present next to 2nd Worcesters. At 2 p.m. an order from Brigade came saying that during the bombardment, prior to the attack, 1st Royal Berks and 1st K.R.R.C. were to send out parties to cut the wire in front of the position to be attacked. At 2.15 p.m. a wire was received saying the attack was suspended and 1st R.Berks were to move back to Old British front line which they did.

At 3.30 p.m. a wire came again ordering the attack on the Quarries at 5.30 p.m. - the order for attack the same as was ordered for 4 p.m. - and at 4 p.m. wire came saying bombardment was to start at 5 p.m. At 5 p.m. the order came to cancel the attack for the day: this came as a great relief to everyone.

1915
Sept.27th
(Contd.)

evening. These orders were subsequently cancelled.

10.30 a.m. Carter's Brigade was ordered to make a fresh attack on the Quarries at 2.30 p.m. 1st Royal Berks. were ordered to pass through Worcester Regiment and the K.R.R. to attack on the left of the Berks, the Worcester Regiment to remain in support.

1.30 p.m. A hostile counter-attack having been successful against the Slag-Heap Fosse No.8. the attack by Carter's Brigade on the 'Quarries' was counter-ordered.

3.0 p.m. British counter-attack on the Slag Heap, Fosse No.8 having been successful, Carter's Brigade was ordered to attack the 'Quarries' at 5.30 p.m.

4.0 p.m. A fresh attack by the enemy against the Slag-Heap Fosse No.8 again driving the British from their position there, the attack on the 'Quarries' was again counter-ordered.

6.0 p.m. Orders received to utilise every man for consolidating the position then held.

11.30 p.m. Orders received by telephone that 1st Royal Berks were to attack the Slag-Heap of Fosse No.8, the attack to take place at 2.30 a.m.

2.30 a.m. 1st Royal Berks were collected from working parties' fatigues, etc. and the attack on the Slag-Heap was launched up to time. The attack failed and

119.

1915
Sept.27th (contd.) the 1st Royal Berks were withdrawn to the Old British front line in rear of 1/K.R.R. and 2nd Worcesters.

9.0 a.m. Colonel Carter was ordered to assume command of 85th Infantry Brigade, and the three Battalions were handed over temporarily to 22nd Inf. Brigade. (see "Carter's Brigade diary")

29th 22nd Inf. Brigade was relieved and 1/K.R.R.C. 1st Royal Berks and 2nd Worcesters returned to 2nd Division.

30th The Battalion arrived in Bethune at 7 a.m. - very tired and dirty. Billets were good, practically everyone asleep all day. On our arrival in the morning the Colonel received a wire from Brigadier General Daly welcoming the Battalion back to the Brigade.

2118.

Page 42

...ence to Appendices

the R...
Rifle Reg. moves

On May

A quiet day - PPCLI relieved
moved back into the B.H. @ huis

May

troops received orders and line to the left taking
over 300 x of trenches from the 28ᵗʰ Div. ((between May 8ᵗʰ)) Appendices
Early quiet day
4 KRR relieved 3 KRR.
3 KRR moved to BHQ line
4 RB replaced 4 KRR in support —

Instructions regarding War Diaries and Intelligence
Summaries are contained in F.S. Regs., Part II.
and the Staff Manual respectively. Title pages
will be prepared in manuscript.

WAR DIARY or INTELLIGENCE SUMMARY

(Erase heading not required.)

Army Form C. 2118

Place	Date	Hour	Summary of Events and Information	Remarks and references to Appendices
Trenches	Sept 28th 1915		Orders were received from the Brigade to notify position of any German Machine Guns in trenches and collections of "derelict arms" so that Salvage Company may be informed, also to endeavour to make a collection of derelict arms and equipment. About 5.30.p.m. the Germans started a very heavy bombing attack on the left flank of "A" Coy. near point "90". At first owing to shortage of bombs on our part they drove us back some forty yards but we managed to check them and finally after two hours heavy bombing we recovered all the lost ground and built up our barricade. 2nd Lieut. L.B.Hall, C.S.M. A.Hopkins and Rfn. Todd threw bombs continuously for more than two hours and it was almost entirely owing to them that the German attack failed. 2nd Lieut. L.B.Hall was completely exhausted, at the finish having strained his heart. We used a great many German bombs in this attack.	2 OR fires
Trenches	Sept 29th 1915		At 5.a.m. the Germans commenced heavy bomb attacks at the same as the previous day, where "D" Coy. had relieved "A". They failed to make any progress and ceased their efforts after about 2 hours. 2nd Lieut. Cayley was killed during this attack. Simultaneously they attacked the barricade in St ELIE AVENUE which was now held by the Worcesters. Here the Germans immediately made progress, partly because the fuses of the Worcesters bombs were wet and would not light. The Worcesters retired in some disorder to where "C" and "B" Coys. were holding the old German line. The Germans who had made a very plucky and well organised attack advanced until they were stopped by heavy rifle fire from our two Companies, and had nearly all their The Germans had come within about twenty yards	

WAR DIARY or INTELLIGENCE SUMMARY

Army Form C. 2118

Place	Date	Hour	Summary of Events and Information	Remarks and references to Appendices
Trenches	Sept 29th continued		of the Old German Front line about 10 men of "C" Coy. went for them with swords fixed and though some of this party were hit by hostile rifle fire from the left. The Germans retired further back. Immediately a supply of bombs had been secured a bombing party from "C" Coy. drove the Germans who seemed to have had enough of it back to their own barricade. We then consolidated our position and strengthened the barricade. A little later the Germans shelled St ELIE AVENUE heavily for half an hour with 4.2 inch and then threw a few bombs but on our replying left us alone for the rest of the day. The barricade was held by our bombers until we were relieved that night by the King's Own, while the Worcesters held the rest of St ELIE AVENUE. All the afternoon there was very heavy bombing near FOSSE 8 and HOHENZOLLERN REDOUBT while urgent requests for bombs and bombers came down every few minutes. We had no bombs to send and of our own bombers who went down to help very few returned. 2nd Lt. J.D.P. Cayley was killed, and 2nd Lt. M.T. Sampson was wounded in the arm, during this attack. Carter's Coy. was relieved by 83rd Brigade at 9pm The Kings Own Regt relieved the Battn about midnight	

6th Infantry Brigade.
2nd Division.

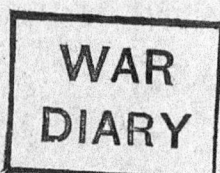

1st BATTN. THE KING'S ROYAL RIFLE CORPSY

OCTOBER

1915

Attached:

Report on Operations
3rd October.

1st Battn. The King's Royal Rifle Corps.

October 1915

Oct. 1st   Lieut.Colonel Armytage had orders to be at the Brigade office at 9 a.m. and did not return until lunch at 1 p.m. with the news that the Brigade would move at 4 p.m. and take over same trenches that we had left the previous morning. The Battalion to relieve the King's Own, and 1st King's on our left. The Battalion moved off at 4 p.m. and was due to relieve at 7 p.m. but owing to an attack Hohenzollern Redoubt - the Hulloch Road was very unhealthy- and we were compelled to get into the trench by the side, and wait for some time, the relief was not completed until 11 p.m. The night was very quiet

1915
Oct. 1st
(Contd.)   on our front, some activity at the Dump and the Redoubt.

2nd   Quiet morning but the Germans shelled us a good
bit in the afternoon, with no damage. Germans were very
active with bombs and shelling in front of the Dump and
Hohenzollern Redoubt all day. At 8.30 p.m. the H.L.I. on
our right attacked to regain a portion of Gun Trench,
which had been lost. This attack was not successful but
while it lasted the Germans shelled us rather unpleasantly
The rest of the night was fairly quiet, no bombing, but
a good bit of sniping.

50. O.R.
Done

3rd   Report of Operations.

About 2.30 p.m. the Germans bombarded our front
lines, support and communication trenches near the
'Quarries' at Vermelles for about 2 hours, with 8" high-
explosive shells - Minenwerfers - and aerial torpedoes,
paying special attention to their old observation post
and Officers dug-outs. During this time we were informed
by the Royal Artillery that the Germans were seen massing
behind their lines, so we were prepared for an attack.
About 4.30 p.m. the Germans started bomb-attacks up the
2 trenches running S.W. from point G.5. D.91. This
attack continued for 2½ hours during which time the
Germans never gained a footing in either of our trenches.

121.

1915
Oct. 3rd
(contd.)

2/Lt E.H. BENTALL D. Coy was killed during the bombardment —

2/Lt K.J.B. ADDY C. Coy was killed during the bomb attack —

On one occasion they attempted to leave theirs, presumably with a view to attacking, but a heavy Rifle and Machine Gun fire was at once opened on them, they did not make a second attempt. We considered our success was entirely due to a properly organised supply of bombs and the steadfastness of the bombers. There were three lines of supplies organised via New Trench from point G.5912 to the V in St.Elie Avenue, also via St.Elie Avenue and via Goeben Avenue.

We expended over 2000 bombs in 2½ hours.

4th   The Battalion arrived and took over billets in the Rue-de-Bruay, Bethune at 5.30 a.m. During the remainder of the day the Battalion rested.

5th   The Battalion spent the day cleaning up and re-fitting clothing.

6th   Brigadier General A.C. Daly came around Company billets at 11.30 a.m. He paid the Battalion this informal visit and congratulated each Company on their excellent work from September 28th to October 3rd.

Lt. A.E. MARSHALL joined the Battalion from 11th Battalion.
2/Lt H.C. PEARSON   "   "   "   "   13th Battalion.

7th   The Battalion still resting in billets. At 10.30 a.m. the Commanding Officer went round billets and complimented the Companies on their excellent work during the past 10

1915
Oct. 7th
(Contd.)   ~~days fighting.~~

The Companies paraded under Os.C. Companies for reconstruction of bombing and Company Training.

8th   The Companies were at the disposal of their Os.C. "A" and "B" Coys. were on the range from 10 a.m. till noon. "C" and "D" Coys. practised bombing and Platoon drill.

At 5.30 p.m. the Battalion received orders to move at once to a place of readiness West of Beuvry on N. of Main Road. This was due to the fact that the Germans were attacking all along the line from Hohenzollern to Loos. The Battalion moved off at 6.40 p.m. The whole Brigade assembled in a large ploughed field just W. of Beuvry on the N. of the Main Road and bivouacked there until 12 midnight when the order came to march back to billets - the German attack having failed with heavy losses to them. The Battalion arrived back at billets about 1 a.m.

Lt A.E. Marshall joined from 1st Batt. posted to A Co
2nd Lt H.C. Kearson   "   13   "   D Co.

9th   The Brigade from 1 a.m. onwards were under 2 hour's notice to move. Coys. were at the disposal of their Os.C. and continued practising - bombing - fire control - and Platoon drill from 10 a.m. to noon.

2/Lt T.N.F. Gibson from 3rd Batt. joined and was posted to C. Coy

Army Form C. 2118

WAR DIARY

Instructions regarding War Diaries and Summaries are contained in F.S. Regulations and the Staff Manual respectively. Will be prepared in manuscript.

Place	Date	Hour		Remarks and references to Appendices
Bethune	Oct 1. 2th 1915		Sunday – Church Parade at noon. No other Parades. At 5 p.m. the Brigade ceased to be under 2 hours notice.	
	13th "	11th	Companies had running parade.	
Bethune			Battalion marched out to trenches near FOUQUEREUIL and practiced blocking and consolidating them against bombing attacks. Brig. Genl. Daly. came up and looked at the work done.	
Bethune	13th "		Companies at disposal O.C.Coys.	
Bethune	14th "		Companies at disposal O.C.Coys. About 5.p.m. the Germans put some 12 inch shells into BETHUNE, the majority falling near the Theatre. The South Staffords had some men knocked out but only some splinters fell near us.	
Bethune / Hingette	15th "		The Brigade was moved out of BETHUNE possibly in consequence of yesterdays shelling. The Battalion marched off at 7.30.a.m. and proceeded to HINGETTE. Very poor billets and there had been some confusion as the South Staffs tried to get into our area.	
Hingette	16th "		Coys. at disposal of O.C.Coys.	
Hingette / Vendin	17th "		The Battalion moved at 8.a.m. to fresh billets at VENDIN, a much better place than HINGETTE.	

WAR DIARY
or
INTELLIGENCE SUMMARY
(Erase heading not required.)

Army Form C. 2118

Place	Date	Hour	Summary of Events and Information	Remarks and references to Appendices
Oct 18th 1915	Fenclin		Church Parade in morning. Orders came in afternoon for the Battalion to be ready to move at once. There had been very heavy artillery fire from the direction of VERMELLES.	
" 19th 1915	Fenclin		Companies paraded for Company drill and instruction in bombing.	
" 20th 1915	Fenclin		Coys. at disposal O.C. Coys.	

Army Form C. 2118.

WAR DIARY
or
INTELLIGENCE SUMMARY.
(Erase heading not required.)

Instructions regarding War Diaries and Intelligence Summaries are contained in F.S. Regs., Part II and the Staff Manual respectively. Title pages will be prepared in manuscript.

Hour, Date, Place	Summary of Events and Information	Remarks and references to Appendices
Oct 21st Vendin Beuvry	Battalion marched from VENDIN to fresh quarters at BEUVRY, still resting. Lieut. A.E. Marshall appointed A/Adjt. vice 2nd Lieut. J. Birkett., the latter being posted to "C" Coy.	
22nd Beuvry	Coys. exercised under Coy. Officers. Battalion Orders announced the award of the Military Cross to 2nd Lieut. L.F. Hall, and the D.C.M. to R/7750. L/Cpl. C. Hendley.	
23rd Beuvry	Coys. exercised under Coy. Officers.	

24th Beuvry
Cuinchy
Cambrin
Ponte Fixe
	Battalion moved into the Support Area, Section A relieving the 1st. King's Regt. Headquarters at HARLEY STREET. Distribution of Battalion in Support Area was as follows:-
	CUINCHY SUPPORT POINT. 2 Platoons of "B" Coy. in Keep
	CAMBRIN " " 1 Platoon of "A" Coy. in Keep and
	                                2 Platoons in occupation.
	PONTE FIXE. S.P. N.BANK. 1 Platoon of "D" Coy. in Keep.
	   " " M.BANK. 3 Platoons of "D" Coy. in occupation.
	   " " S.BANK. 1 Platoon of "C" Coy. in Keep.
	   " " S.BANK. 3 Platoons of "C" Coy. in occupation.
	                               2 Platoons of "B" Coy. and 1 of "A"
	CAMBRIN VILLAGE. in occupation.
	The Battalion was occupied mostly in supplying working parties for the improvement of trenches under the direction of the R.E.	

Army Form C. 2118.

WAR DIARY
or
INTELLIGENCE SUMMARY.
(Erase heading not required.)

Instructions regarding War Diaries and Intelligence Summaries are contained in F.S. Regs., Part II and the Staff Manual respectively. Title pages will be prepared in manuscript.

Hour, Date, Place	Summary of Events and Information	Remarks and references to Appendices
Oct. 25th. Cuinchy { Cambrin Pont Fixe }	Battalion worked on improvement of its own quarters, the working parties ordered not being able to work on account of inclement weather.	
26th. Cuinchy { Cambrin Pont Fixe }	Battalion fully employed on working parties, every available man having to be turned out to find 2 parties of 320 men.	
27th. Cuinchy.	Battalion was relieved in the Support Area by the 5th. Liverpool Regt. at 2.20.p.m. and moved up to the front line trenches relieving the 1st. King's Regt. about 3.30.p.m. The distribution was:-	
	"A" Coy. and 1 Platoon of "B"	RIDLEY WALK (excl.) to HANOVER St. (incl.) BRICKSTACK KEEP and BRICKSTACK TERRACE.
	"C" Coy.	HANOVER St. (excl.) to DAVIES St. (incl.) BRICKSTACK TERRACE LEICESTER Sq. and PETTICOAT LANE.
	"D" Coy.	DAVIES St. ( ) to CAN( ) and HUNTER St.
	"B" Coy. (less 1 Platoon.)	ESPERANTO TERRACE, PUDDLING LANE, BATH St. CABBAGE PATCH REDOUBT, and LOVERS REDOUBT.
	Capt. T.G. Dalby joined the Battalion from ETAPLES, and took over the duties of Second in Command.	

Army Form C. 2118.

WAR DIARY
or
INTELLIGENCE SUMMARY.
(Erase heading not required.)

Instructions regarding War Diaries and Intelligence Summaries are contained in F.S. Regs., Part II. and the Staff Manual respectively. Title pages will be prepared in manuscript.

Hour, Date, Place	Summary of Events and Information	Remarks and references to Appendices
Oct 28th. Cuinchy.	The first night in the trenches passed quietly, no hostile artillery fire, very little trench mortar, and only intermittent rifle fire by snipers. A considerable amount of work was done on improvement of trenches. Weather on 28th. very wet. Trenches in bad condition. The only casualty was 4453 Rfn Gosford Killed by sniper. (Head, bullet.) He was killed about 10.30.a.m. on the 28th. and was buried in VOGUED CUINCHY ABBEY CEMETERY at 3.p.m. His Majesty the King inspected detachments of the First Army during the day. At this inspection the Battalion was represented by 2 N.C.O's. and 25 men (taken from the Transport) under the command of 2nd. Lieut Allfrey.	
29th Cuinchy.	Still in trenches. Enemy shelled & bombed with trench mortar guns men wounded. (One slightly from shock.) Worked on improvement of trenches. G.O.C. First Corps Army visited the trenches.	
30th Cuinchy.	Relieved in Section A.2. by South Staffordshire Regt. about 12.30 p.m One casualty on morning of 30th. Bullet graze in head. town Enemy was on the whole inactive during this town. After relief the Battalion marched to ANNEQUIN to billets 2nd. Lieut I.M. Harris joined the Battalion	

(73989) W4141—463. 400,000. 9/14. H.&J.Ltd. Forms/C. 2118/10.

Oct 31st Annequin.	In billets at ANNEQUIN supplying working parties for cleaning etc., of trenches. Whilst one of these parties was waiting for the remainder to join them preparatory to marching off some of the party picked up a German rifle grenade which they took to a dug-out. ~~In the subsequent messing about~~ The grenade exploded whilst the men were handling it and the ensuing casualties were:- 1 O.R. killed, 1 died of wounds, 6 wounded.

REPORT ON OPERATIONS 3RD OCTOBER.

Report on Operations, 3rd October, 1915.

About 2.30.p.m. on October 3rd, the Germans bombarded our Front Lines, Support and Communication Trenches, near the QUARRIES at VERMELLES, for about 2 hours with 8" high explosive shells, Minnewerfers and Aerial Torpedoes, paying special attention to their old Observation Post and Officers' dug-outs.

During this time I was informed by the Royal Artillery that the Germans were seen massing behind their lines, so was prepared for an attack.

About 4.30.p.m. the Germans started bomb attacks up the trenches running S.W. from Point G.5.d.9.1. This attack continued for 2½ hours, during which time the Germans never gained a footing in either of our trenches.

On one occasion they attempted to leave theirs presumably with a view to attacking, but a heavy rifle and machine gun fire was at once opened on them and they did not make a second attempt.

I consider our success was entirely due to "a properly organised supply of bombs" and the steadfastness of the Bombers.

There were three lines of supplies organised via NEW TRENCH from Point G.5.9.1.2. to the V in ST. ELIE AVENUE, also via ST. ELIE AVENUE.

We expended over 2000 bombs in 2½ hours.

4.10.15.   Sd.   G.A.ARMYTAGE,   Major,
                      Commanding 1st K.R.Rifle Corps.

1st BATTALION, KING'S ROYAL RIFLE CORPS.

1915
October

Appendix.

1st   Lieut. Colonel Armytage had orders to be at the Brigade office at 9 a.m. and did not return until lunch at 1 p.m. with the news that the Brigade would move at 4 p.m. and take over same trenches that we had left the previous morning. The Battalion to relieve the King's Own, and 1st King's on our left. The Battalion moved off at 4 pm. and was due to relieve at 7 p.m. but owing to an attack Hohenzollern Redoubt - the Hulloch Road was very unhealthy - and we were compelled to get into the trench by the side, and wait for some time, the relief was not completed until 11 p.m.
The night was very quiet on our front, some activity at the Dump and the Redoubt.

2nd   Quiet morning but the Germans shelled us a good bit in the afternoon, with no damage. Germans were very active with bombs and shelling in front of the Dump and Hohenzollern Redoubt all day. At 8.30 p.m. the H.L.I. on our right attacked to regain a portion of Gun Trench which had been lost. This attack was not successful but while it lasted the Germans shelled us rather unpleasantly. The rest of the night was fairly quiet, no bombing, but a good bit of sniping.

3rd   Report of Operations.
About 2.30 p.m. the Germans bombarded our front lines, support and communication trenches near the "Quarries" at Vermelles for about 2 hours, with 8" high explosive shells - Minenwerfers - and aerial torpedoes, paying special attention to their old observation post and Officers' dug-outs. During this time we were informed by the Royal Artillery

1915   Appendix.

October

3rd (C'td.) — that the Germans were seen massing behind their lines, so we were prepared for an attack. About 4.30 p.m. the Germans started bomb-attacks up the 2 trenches running S.W. from point G.5. D.91. This attack continued for 2½ hours during which time the Germans never gained a footing in either of our trenches. On one occasion they attempted to leave theirs, presumably with a view to attacking, but a hravy Rifle and Machine Gun fire was at once opened on them, they did not make a second attempt. We considered our success was entirely due to a properly organised supply of bombs and the steadfastness of the bombers. There were three lines of supplies organised via New Trench from point G.5912 to the V in St. Elie Avenue, also via St. Elie Avenue and via Goeben Avenue. We expended over 2,000 bombs in 2½ hours.
2nd Lt. E.H. Bentall, D Co. was killed during bombardment.
2nd Lt. K.T. Boddy, C Co. was killed during the bombardment.

4th — The Battalion arrived and took over billets in the Rue-de-Bruay, Bethune at 5.30 a.m. During the remainder of the day the Battalion rested.

5th — The Battalion spent the day cleaning up and refitting clothing.

6th — Brigadier General A.C. Daly came around Company billets at 11.30am. He paid the Battalion this informal visit and congratulated each Company on their excellent work from September 28th to October 3rd.

7th — The Battalion still resting in Billets.
The Companies paraded under O.C's Companies for reconstruction of bombing and Company Training.

8th — The Companies were at the disposal of their O's C. "A" and "B" Coys. were on the range from 10 a.m. till noon. "C" and "D" Coys. practised bombing and Platoon drill.

1915   Appendix.

October

8th
(C'td.)
At 5.30 p.m. the Battalion received orders to move at once to a place of readiness West of Beuvry on N. side of Main Road. This was due to the fact that the Germans were attacking all along the line from Hohenzollern to Loos. The Battalion moved off at 6.40pm. The whole Brigade assembled in a large ploughed field just W. of Beuvry on the N. of the Main Road and bivouacked there until 12 midnight when the order came to march back to billets - the German attack having failed with heavy losses to them. The Battalion arrived back at billets about 1 a.m.
Lt. A.E. Marshall joined from 4th Battn. & posted to "A" Coy.
2 Lt. Rennan from 18th (ex 13th) Battn posted to D. Co.

9th
The Brigade from 1 a.m. onwards were under 2 hours' notice to move. Coys were at the disposal of their Os. C. and continued practising - bombing - fire control - and Platoon drill from 10 a.m. to noon.
2nd Lt. T.N.F. Wilson from 3rd Battn joined & was posted to C. Co.

10th
Sunday - Church Parade at noon.
No other Parades.
At 5 p.m. the Brigade ceased to be under 2 hours notice.

11th
Companies had running parade.

BETHUNE.

12th
Battalion marched out to trenches near FOUQUEREUIL and practised blocking and consolidating them against bombing attacks.
Brig. General Daly came up and looked at the work done.

13th
Companies at disposal of O.C. Coys.

14th
Companies at disposal of O.C. Coys.
About 5 p.m. the Germans put some 12 inch shells into BETHUNE, the majority falling near the Theatre. The South Staffords had some men knocked out but only some splinters fell near us.

Appendix.

1915

October — BETHUNE - HINGETTE.

15th   The Brigade was moved out of BETHUNE possibly in consequence of yesterday's shelling. The Battalion marched off at 7.30am. and proceeded to HINGETTE. Very poor billets and there had been some confusion as the South Staffs tried to get into our area.

HINGETTE.

16th   Coys. at disposal of O.Cs Coys.

HINGETTE - VENDIN.

17th   The Battalion moved at 8 a.m. to fresh billets at VENDIN, a much better place than HINGETTE.

VENDIN.

18th   Church Parade in morning. Orders came in the afternoon for the Battalion to be ready to move at once. There had been very heavy artillery fire from the direction of VERMELLES.

19th   Companies paraded for Coy. Drill and instruction in bombing.

20th   Coys at disposal of O.C. Coys.

VENDIN - BEUVRY.

21st   Battalion marched from VENDIN to fresh quarters at BEUVRY, still resting. Lieut. A.E. Marshall appointed A/Adjt. vice 2nd Lieut. C. Birkett, the latter being posted to "C" Coy.

BEUVRY.

22nd   Coys exercised under Coy. Officers. Battalion orders announced the award of the Military Cross to 2nd Lieut. L. E. Hall, and the D.C.M. to R/7750 L/Cpl. C. Hendley.

23rd   Coys exercised under Coy. Officers.

Appendix.

1915

October 24th — BEUVRY - CUINCHY, CAMBRIN, PONTE FIXE.
Battalion moved into the Support Area, Section A relieving the 1st King's Regt. Headquarters at HARLEY STREET. Distribution of Battalion in Support Area was as follows:-
CUINCHY SUPPORT POINT -
2 Platoons of "B" Coy. in Keep.
CAMBRIN SUPPORT POINT -
1 Platoon of "A" Coy. in Keep & 2 Platoons in occupation.
PONTE FIXE, S.P. N. BANK -
1 Platoon of "D" Coy. in Keep.
" " S.P. N. BANK -
3 Platoons of D Coy. in occupation.
" " S.P. S. BANK -
1 Platoon of C Coy. in Keep.
" " S.P. S. BANK. -
3 Platoons of "C" Coy. in occupation.
CAMBRIN VILLAGE -
2 Platoons of B Coy. and 1 of "A" in occupation.
The Battalion was occupied mostly in supplying working parties for the improvement of trenches under the direction of the R.E.

CUINCHY - CAMBRIN - PONTE FIXE.

25th Battalion worked on improvement of its own quarters, the working parties ordered not being able to work on account of inclement weather.

26th Battalion fully employed on working parties, every available man having to be turned out to find 2 parties of 320 men.

27th CUINCHY.
Battalion was relieved in the Support Area by the 5th Liverpool Regt. at 2.20 p.m. and moved up to the front line trenches relieving the 1st King's Regt. about 3.30 p.m.
The distribution was:- "A" Coy. and 1 Platoon of "B" - RIDLEY WALK (excl) to HANOVER ST. (incl.) BRICKSTACK KEEP and BRICKSTACK TERRACE.
"C" Coy. HANOVER ST. (excl) to DAVIES ST. (incl.) BRICKSTACK TERRACE, LEICESTER SQ. and PETTICOAT LANE.
"D" Coy. DAVIES ST. (excl.) to CANADA and HUNTER ST.
"B" Coy. (less 1 Platoon) ESPERANTO TERRACE, PUDDING LANE, BATH ST. CABBAGE PATCH REDOUBT & LOVERS REDOUBT.

1915   Appendix.

October

27th   Capt. T.G. Dalby joined the
(C'td.)   Battalion from ETAPLES and took
          over the duties of Second in
          Command.

28th   The first night in the trenches
          passed quietly, no hostile
          artillery fire, very little
          trench mortar and only inter-
          mittent rifle fire by snipers.
          A considerable amount of work
          was done on improvement of
          trenches. Weather on 28th very
          wet. Trenches in bad condition.
          The only casualty was No.4433 Rfn.
          Cosford killed by sniper. (Head,
          bullet) He was killed about
          10.30 a.m. on the 28th and was
          buried in WOBURN ABBEY CEMETERY
          at 3 p.m.
          His Majesty the King inspected
          detachments of the first Army
          during the day. At this inspection
          the Battalion was represented by
          2 N.C.O's and 26 men (taken from
          the Transport) under the command
          of 2nd Lieut. Allfrey.

29th   Still in trenches. Enemy shelled
          & bombed with trench mortar.
          Four men wounded (one slightly from
          shock). Worked on improvement of
          trenches. G.O.C. First Corps
          visited the trenches.
          CUINCHY - ANNEQUIN.

30th   Relieved in Section A.2. by South
          Staffordshire Regt. about 12.30pm.
          One casualty on morning of 30th.
          Bullet graze in head. Enemy was
          on the whole inactive during this
          tour. After relief the Battalion
          marched to ANNEQUIN to billets.
          2nd Lieut. I.M. Harris joined the
          Battalion.

          ANNEQUIN.

31st   In billets at ANNEQUIN supplying
          working parties for cleaning etc.
          of trenches. Whilst one of these
          parties was waiting for the
          remainder to join them preparatory
          to marching off some of the party
          picked up a German rifle grenade
          which they took to a dug-out.
          The grenade exploded whilst the
          men were handling it and the ensuing
          casualties were :- 1 O.R. killed,
          1 died of wounds, 6 wounded.

When marking

When marking

1st BATTALION, KING'S ROYAL RIFLE CORPS.

1915 Appendix.
October

1st   Lieut. Colonel Armytage had orders to be at the Brigade office at 9 a.m. and did not return until lunch at 1 p.m. with the news that the Brigade would move at 4 p.m. and take over same trenches that we had left the previous morning. The Battalion to relieve the King's Own, and 1st King's on our left. The Battalion moved off at 4 pm. and was due to relieve at 7 p.m. but owing to an attack Hohenzollern Redoubt - the Hulloch Road was very unhealthy - and we were compelled to get into the trench by the side, and wait for some time, the relief was not completed until 11 p.m.
The night was very quiet on our front, some activity at the Dump and the Redoubt.

2nd   Quiet morning but the Germans shelled us a good bit in the afternoon, with no damage. Germans were very active with bombs and shelling in front of the Dump and Hohenzollern Redoubt all day. At 8.30 p.m. the H.L.I. on our right attacked to regain a portion of Gun Trench which had been lost. This attack was not successful but while it lasted the Germans shelled us rather unpleasantly. The rest of the night was fairly quiet, no bombing, but a good bit of sniping.

3rd   Report of Operations.
About 2.30 p.m. the Germans bombarded our front lines, support and communication trenches near the "Quarries" at Vermelles for about 2 hours, with 8" high explosive shells - Minenwerfers - and aerial torpedoes, paying special attention to their old observation post and Officers' dug-outs. During this time we were informed by the Royal Artillery

1915 Appendix.

October

3rd (C'td.) that the Germans were seen massing behind their lines, so we were prepared for an attack. About 4.30 p.m. the Germans started bomb-attacks up the 2 trenches running S.W. from point G.5. D.91. This attack continued for 2½ hours during which time the Germans never gained a footing in either of our trenches. On one occasion they attempted to leave theirs, presumably with a view to attacking, but a heavy Rifle and Machine Gun fire was at once opened on them, they did not make a second attempt. We considered our success was entirely due to a properly organised supply of bombs and the steadfastness of the bombers. There were three lines of supplies organised via New Trench from point G.5912 to the Y in St. Elie Avenue, also via St. Elie Avenue and via Goeben Avenue. We expended over 2,000 bombs in 2½ hours.
2nd Lt. E.H. Bentall, D Co. was killed during bombardment.
2nd Lt. K.T. Eddy, C Co. was killed during the bombardment.

4th The Battalion arrived and took over billets in the Rue-de-Bruay, Bethune at 5.30 a.m. During the remainder of the day the Battalion rested.

5th The Battalion spent the day cleaning up and refitting clothing.

6th Brigadier General A.C. Daly came around Company billets at 11.30am. He paid the Battalion this informal visit and congratulated each Company on their excellent work from September 28th to October 3rd.

7th The Battalion still resting in Billets.
The Companies paraded under O.C's Companies for reconstruction of bombing and Company Training.

8th The Companies were at the disposal of their O's C. "A" and "B" Coys. were on the range from 10 a.m. till noon. "C" and "D" Coys. practised bombing and Platoon drill.

1915   Appendix.

October

8th   At 5.30 p.m. the Battalion
(C'td.)   received orders to move at once
            to a place of readiness West of
            Beuvry on N. side of Main Road.
            This was due to the fact that the
            Germans were attacking all along
            the line from Hohenzollern to Loos.
            The Battalion moved off at 6.40pm.
            The whole Brigade assembled in a
            large ploughed field just W. of
            Beuvry on the N. of the Main Road
            and bivouacked there until 12 mid-
            night when the order came to march
            back to billets - the German attack
            having failed with heavy losses to
            them. The Battalion arrived back
            at billets about 1 a.m.
            Lt. A.E. Marshall joined from 4th
            Battn. & posted to "A" Coy.
            2 Lt. Rennan from 18th (ex 13th)
            Battn posted to D. Co.

9th   The Brigade from 1 a.m. onwards
            were under 2 hours' notice to move.
            Coys were at the disposal of their
            Os. C. and continued practising -
            bombing - fire control - and Platoon
            drill from 10 a.m. to noon.
            2nd Lt. T.E.F. Wilson from 3rd Battn
            joined & was posted to C. Co.

10th   Sunday - Church Parade at noon.
            No other Parades.
            At 5 p.m. the Brigade ceased to be
            under 2 hours notice.

11th   Companies had running parade.

            BETHUNE.

12th   Battalion marched out to trenches
            near FOUQUEREUIL and practised
            blocking and consolidating them
            against bombing attacks.
            Brig. General Daly came up and
            looked at the work done.

13th   Companies at disposal of O.C. Coys.

14th   Companies at disposal of O.C. Coys.
            About 5 p.m. the Germans put some
            12 inch shells into BETHUNE, the
            majority falling near the Theatre.
            The South Staffords had some men
            knocked out but only some splinters
            fell near us.

1915 Appendix.

October BETHUNE - HINGETTE.

15th The Brigade was moved out of BETHUNE possibly in consequence of yesterday's shelling. The Battalion marched off at 7.30am. and proceeded to HINGETTE. Very poor billets and there had been some confusion as the South Staffs tried to get into our area.

HINGETTE.

16th Coys. at disposal of O.Cs Coys.

HINGETTE - VENDIN.

17th The Battalion moved at 8 a.m. to fresh billets at VENDIN, a much better place than HINGETTE.

VENDIN.

18th Church Parade in morning. Orders came in the afternoon for the Battalion to be ready to move at once. There had been very heavy artillery fire from the direction of VERMELLES.

19th Companies paraded for Coy. Drill and instruction in bombing.

20th Coys at disposal of O.C. Coys.

VENDIN - BEUVRY.

21st Battalion marched from VENDIN to fresh quarters at BEUVRY, still resting. Lieut. A.E. Marshall appointed A/Adjt. vice 2nd Lieut. C. Birkett, the latter being posted to "C" Coy.

BEUVRY.

22nd Coys exercised under Coy. Officers. Battalion orders announced the award of the Military Cross to 2nd Lieut. L. E. Hall, and the D.C.M. to R/7750 L/Cpl. C.Hendley.

23rd Coys exercised under Coy. Officers.

Appendix.

1915

October	**BEUVRY - CUINCHY CAMBRIN PONTE FIXE.**
24th	Battalion moved into the Support Area, Section A relieving the 1st King's Regt. Headquarters at HARLEY STREET. Distribution of Battalion in Support Area was as follows:-

CUINCHY SUPPORT POINT -
2 Platoons of "B" Coy. in Keep.
CAMBRIN SUPPORT POINT -
1 Platoon of "A" Coy. in Keep &
2 Platoons in occupation.
PONTE FIXE. S.P. N. BANK -
    1 Platoon of "D" Coy.
    in Keep.
"   " S.P. N. BANK -
    3 Platoons of D Coy.
    in occupation.
"   " S.P. S. BANK -
    1 Platoon of C Coy.
    in Keep.
"   " S.P. S. BANK.-
    3 Platoons of "C" Coy.
    in occupation.
CAMBRIN VILLAGE -
2 Platoons of B Coy. and 1 of "A"
in occupation.
The Battalion was occupied mostly in supplying working parties for the improvement of trenches under the direction of the R.E.

CUINCHY - CAMBRIN - PONTE FIXE.

25th	Battalion worked on improvement of its own quarters, the working parties ordered not being able to work on account of inclement weather.
26th	Battalion fully employed on working parties, every available man having to be turned out to find 2 parties of 320 men.
27th	**CUINCHY.** Battalion was relieved in the Support Area by the 5th Liverpool Regt. at 2.20 p.m. and moved up to the front line trenches relieving the 1st King's Regt. about 3.30 p.m. The distribution was:- "A" Coy. and 1 Platoon of "B" - RIDLEY WALK (excl) to HANOVER ST. (incl.) BRICKSTACK KEEP and BRICKSTACK TERRACE. "C" Coy. HANOVER ST. (excl) to DAVIES ST. (incl.) BRICKSTACK TERRACE, LEICESTER SQ. and PETTICOAT LANE. "D" Coy. DAVIES ST. (excl.) to CANADA and HUNTER ST. "B" Coy. (less 1 Platoon) ESPERANTO TERRACE, PUDDING LANE, BATH ST. CABBAGE PATCH REDOUBT & LOVERS REDOUBT.

1915   Appendix.

October

27th (C'td.) — Capt. T.G. Dalby joined the Battalion from ETAPLES and took over the duties of Second in Command.

28th — The first night in the trenches passed quietly, no hostile artillery fire, very little trench mortar and only intermittent rifle fire by snipers. A considerable amount of work was done on improvement of trenches. Weather on 28th very wet. Trenches in bad condition. The only casualty was No.4433 Rfn. Cosford killed by sniper. (Head, bullet) He was killed about 10.30 a.m. on the 28th and was buried in WOBURN ABBEY CEMETERY at 3 p.m.
His Majesty the King inspected detachments of the first Army during the day. At this inspection the Battalion was represented by 2 N.C.O's and 26 men (taken from the Transport) under the command of 2nd Lieut. Allfrey.

29th — Still in trenches. Enemy shelled & bombed with trench mortar. Four men wounded (one slightly from shock). Worked on improvement of trenches. G.O.C. First Corps visited the trenches.

CUINCHY - ANNEQUIN.

30th — Relieved in Section A.2. by South Staffordshire Regt. about 12.30pm. One casualty on morning of 30th. Bullet graze in head. Enemy was on the whole inactive during this tour. After relief the Battalion marched to ANNEQUIN to billets. 2nd Lieut. I.M. Harris joined the Battalion.

ANNEQUIN.

31st — In billets at ANNEQUIN supplying working parties for cleaning etc. of trenches. Whilst one of these parties was waiting for the remainder to join them preparatory to marching off some of the party picked up a German rifle grenade which they took to a dug-out. The grenade exploded whilst the men were handling it and the ensuing casualties were :- 1 O.R. killed, 1 died of wounds, 6 wounded.

1st BATTALION, KING'S ROYAL RIFLE CORPS.

1915 Appendix.

October

1st Lieut. Colonel Armytage had orders to be at the Brigade office at 9 a.m. and did not return until lunch at 1 p.m. with the news that the Brigade would move at 4 p.m. and take over same trenches that we had left the previous morning. The Battalion to relieve the King's Own, and 1st King's on our left. The Battalion moved off at 4 p.m. and was due to relieve at 7 p.m. but owing to an attack Hohenzollern Redoubt - the Bulloch Road was very unhealthy - and we were compelled to get into the trench by the side, and wait for some time, the relief was not completed until 11 p.m.
The night was very quiet on our front, some activity at the Dump and the Redoubt.

2nd Quiet morning but the Germans shelled us a good bit in the afternoon, with no damage. Germans were very active with bombs and shelling in front of the Dump and Hohenzollern Redoubt all day. At 8.30 p.m. the H.L.I. on our right attacked to regain a portion of Gun Trench which had been lost. This attack was not successful but while it lasted the Germans shelled us rather unpleasantly. The rest of the night was fairly quiet, no bombing, but a good bit of sniping.

3rd Report of Operations.
About 2.30 p.m. the Germans bombarded our front lines, support and communication trenches near the "Quarries" at Vermelles for about 2 hours, with 8" high explosive shells - Minenwerfers - and aerial torpedoes, paying special attention to their old observation post and Officers' dug-outs. During this time we were informed by the Royal Artillery

1915   Appendix.

October

3rd
(C'td.)   that the Germans were seen massing
          behind their lines, so we were
          prepared for an attack. About
          4.30 p.m. the Germans started bomb-
          attacks up the 2 trenches running
          S.W. from point G.5.D.91. This
          attack continued for 2½ hours
          during which time the Germans never
          gained a footing in either of our
          trenches. On one occasion they
          attempted to leave theirs, presumably
          with a view to attacking, but a
          heavy Rifle and Machine Gun fire
          was at once opened on them, they did
          not make a second attempt. We
          considered our success was entirely
          due to a properly organised supply
          of bombs and the steadfastness of
          the bombers. There were three
          lines of supplies organised via
          New Trench from point G.5912 to the
          Y in St. Elie Avenue, also via
          St. Elie Avenue and via Goeben
          Avenue. We expended over 2,000
          bombs in 2½ hours.
          2nd Lt. E.R. Bentall, D Co. was
          killed during bombardment.
          2nd Lt. K.T. Boddy, C Co. was
          killed during the bombardment.

4th   The Battalion arrived and took over
          billets in the Rue-de-Bruay, Bethune
          at 5.30 a.m. During the remainder
          of the day the Battalion rested.

5th   The Battalion spent the day clear-
          ing up and refitting clothing.

6th   Brigadier General A.C. Daly came
          around Company billets at 11.30am.
          He paid the Battalion this informal
          visit and congratulated each Company
          on their excellent work from
          September 28th to October 3rd.

7th   The Battalion still resting in
          Billets.
          The Companies paraded under O.C's
          Companies for reconstruction of
          bombing and Company Training.

8th   The Companies were at the disposal
          of their O's C. "A" and "B" Coys.
          were on the range from 10 a.m. till
          noon. "C" and "D" Coys. practised
          bombing and Platoon drill.

1915   Appendix.

October

8th (C'td.) — At 8.30 p.m. the Battalion received orders to move at once to a place of readiness West of Beuvry on N. side of Main Road. This was due to the fact that the Germans were attacking all along the line from Hohenzollern to Loos. The Battalion moved off at 8.40pm. The whole Brigade assembled in a large ploughed field just W. of Beuvry on the N. of the Main Road and bivouacked there until 12 midnight when the order came to march back to billets – the German attack having failed with heavy losses to them. The Battalion arrived back at billets about 1 a.m.
Lt. A.E. Marshall joined from 4th Battn. & posted to "A" Coy.
2 Lt. Renman from 18th (ex 13th) Battn posted to D. Co.

9th — The Brigade from 1 a.m. onwards were under 2 hours' notice to move. Coys were at the disposal of their On. C. and continued practising – bombing – fire control – and Platoon drill from 10 a.m. to noon.
2nd Lt. T.E.F. Wilson from 3rd Battn joined & was posted to C. Co.

10th — Sunday – Church Parade at noon. No other Parades.
At 5 p.m. the Brigade ceased to be under 2 hours notice.

11th — Companies had running parade.

BETHUNE.

12th — Battalion marched out to trenches near FOUQUEREUIL and practised blocking and consolidating them against bombing attacks.
Brig. General Daly came up and looked at the work done.

13th — Companies at disposal of O.C. Coys.

14th — Companies at disposal of O.C. Coys. About 5 p.m. the Germans put some 12 inch shells into BETHUNE, the majority falling near the Theatre. The South Staffords had some men knocked out but only some splinters fell near us.

1915   Appendix.

October   BETHUNE - HINGETTE.

15th   The Brigade was moved out of
           BETHUNE possibly in consequence
           of yesterday's shelling. The
           Battalion marched off at 7.30am.
           and proceeded to HINGETTE. Very
           poor billets and there had been
           some confusion as the South
           Staffs tried to get into our
           area.

           HINGETTE.

16th   Coys. at disposal of O.Cs Coys.

           HINGETTE - VENDIN.

17th   The Battalion moved at 6 a.m.
           to fresh billets at VENDIN, a
           much better place than HINGETTE.

           VENDIN.

18th   Church Parade in morning.
           Orders came in the afternoon
           for the Battalion to be ready to
           move at once. There had been
           very heavy artillery fire from
           the direction of VERMELLES.

19th   Companies paraded for Coy. Drill
           and instruction in bombing.

20th   Coys at disposal of O.C. Coys.

           VENDIN - BEUVRY.

21st   Battalion marched from VENDIN
           to fresh quarters at BEUVRY, still
           resting. Lieut. A.E. Marshall
           appointed A/Adjt. vice 2nd Lieut.
           C. Birkett, the latter being posted
           to "C" Coy.

           BEUVRY.

22nd   Coys exercised under Coy. Officers.
           Battalion orders announced the
           award of the Military Cross to
           2nd Lieut. L. E. Hall, and the
           D.C.M. to R/7750 L/Cpl. C.Hendley.

23rd   Coys exercised under Coy. Officers.

Appendix.

1915

October
24th   BEUVRY - GUINCHY CAMBRIN POSTE
            FIXE.
            Battalion moved into the Support
            Area, Section A relieving the 1st
            King's Regt. Headquarters at
            HARLEY STREET. Distribution of
            Battalion in Support Area was as
            follows:-
            GUINCHY SUPPORT POINT -
            3 Platoons of "B" Coy. in Keep.
            CAMBRIN SUPPORT POINT -
            1 Platoon of "A" Coy. in Keep &
            3 Platoons in occupation.
            POSTE FIXE. A.P. N. BANK -
                        1 Platoon of "D" Coy.
                        in Keep.
               "   "   A.P. N. BANK -
                        3 Platoons of D Coy.
                        in occupation.
               "   "   A.P. S. BANK -
                        1 Platoon of C Coy.
                        in Keep.
               "   "   A.P. S. BANK -
                        3 Platoons of "C" Coy.
                        in occupation.
            CAMBRIN VILLAGE -
            2 Platoons of B Coy. and 1 of "A"
            in occupation.
            The Battalion was occupied mostly
            in supplying working parties for
            the improvement of trenches under
            the direction of the R.E.

            GUINCHY - CAMBRIN - POSTE FIXE.

25th   Battalion worked on improvement of
            its own quarters, the working parties
            ordered not being able to work on
            account of inclement weather.

26th   Battalion fully employed on working
            parties, every available man having
            to be turned out to find 2 parties
            of 320 men.

            GUINCHY

27th   Battalion was relieved in the Support
            Area by the 5th Liverpool Regt. at
            2.20 p.m. and moved up to the front
            line trenches relieving the 1st King's
            Regt. about 3.20 p.m.
            The distribution was:- "A" Coy. and
            1 Platoon of "B" - REBURY WALK (excl)
            to HANOVER ST. (incl.) BRICKSTACK
            KEEP and BRICKSTACK TERRACE.
            "C" Coy. HANOVER ST. (excl) to DAVIES
            ST. (incl.) BRICKSTACK TERRACE,
            LEICESTER SQ. and PETTICOAT LANE.
            "D" Coy. DAVIES ST. (excl.) to CANADA
            and HUNTER ST.
            "B" Coy. (less 1 Platoon) ESPERANTO
            TERRACE, PUDDING LANE, BATH ST, CABBAGE PATCH
            REDOUBT & LOVERS REDOUBT.

1915   Appendix.

October

27th
(C'td.)   Capt. T.G. Dalby joined the
           Battalion from ETAPLES and took
           over the duties of Second in
           Command.

28th   The first night in the trenches
           passed quietly, no hostile
           artillery fire, very little
           trench mortar and only inter-
           mittent rifle fire by snipers.
           A considerable amount of work
           was done on improvement of
           trenches. Weather on 28th very
           wet. Trenches in bad condition.
           The only casualty was No.4433 Rfn.
           Cosford killed by sniper. (Head,
           bullet) He was killed about
           10.30 a.m. on the 28th and was
           buried in WOBURN ABBEY CEMETERY
           at 3 p.m.
           His Majesty the King inspected
           detachments of the first Army
           during the day. At this inspection
           the Battalion was represented by
           2 N.C.O's and 26 men (taken from
           the Transport) under the command
           of 2nd Lieut. Allfrey.

29th   Still in trenches. Enemy shelled
           & bombed with trench mortar.
           Four men wounded (one slightly from
           shock). Worked on improvement of
           trenches. G.O.C. First Corps
           visited the trenches.
           CUINCHY - ANNEQUIN.

30th   Relieved in Section A.2. by South
           Staffordshire Regt. about 12.30pm.
           One casualty on morning of 30th.
           Bullet graze in head. Enemy was
           on the whole inactive during this
           tour. After relief the Battalion
           marched to ANNEQUIN to billets.
           2nd Lieut. I.R. Harris joined the
           Battalion.

           ANNEQUIN.

31st   In billets at ANNEQUIN supplying
           working parties for cleaning etc.
           of trenches. Whilst one of these
           parties was waiting for the
           remainder to join them preparatory
           to marching off some of the party
           picked up a German rifle grenade
           which they took to a dug-out.
           The grenade exploded whilst the
           men were handling it and the ensuing
           casualties were :- 1 O.R. killed,
           1 died of wounds, 6 wounded.

1st BATTALION, KING'S ROYAL RIFLE CORPS.

1915   Appendix.

October

1st   Lieut. Colonel Armytage had
         orders to be at the Brigade
         office at 9 a.m. and did not
         return until lunch at 1 p.m.
         with the news that the Brigade
         would move at 4 p.m. and take
         over same trenches that we had
         left the previous morning. The
         Battalion to relieve the King's
         Own, and 1st King's on our left.
         The Battalion moved off at 4 p.m.
         and was due to relieve at 7 p.m.
         but owing to an attack Hohen-
         zollern Redoubt - the Bulloch
         Road was very unhealthy - and we
         were compelled to get into the
         trench by the side, and wait for
         some time, the relief was not
         completed until 11 p.m.
         The night was very quiet on our
         front, some activity at the Dump
         and the Redoubt.

2nd   Quiet morning but the Germans
         shelled us a good bit in the
         afternoon, with no damage.
         Germans were very active with
         bombs and shelling in front of
         the Dump and Hohenzollern Redoubt
         all day. At 8.30 p.m. the H.L.I.
         on our right attacked to regain a
         portion of Gun Trench which had
         been lost. This attack was not
         successful but while it lasted
         the Germans shelled us rather
         unpleasantly. The rest of the
         night was fairly quiet, no bombing,
         but a good bit of sniping.

3rd   **Report of Operations.**
         About 2.30 p.m. the Germans
         bombarded our front lines, support
         and communication trenches near
         the "Quarries" at Vermelles for
         about 2 hours, with 8" high
         explosive shells - Minenwerfers -
         and aerial torpedoes, paying
         special attention to their old
         observation post and Officers'
         dug-outs. During this time we
         were informed by the Royal Artillery

1915   Appendix.
October

3rd   that the Germans were seen massing
(C'td.)   behind their lines, so we were
             prepared for an attack. About
             4.30 p.m. the Germans started bomb-
             attacks up the 2 trenches running
             S.W. from point G.S. D.61. This
             attack continued for 2½ hours
             during which time the Germans never
             gained a footing in either of our
             trenches. On one occasion they
             attempted to leave theirs, presumably
             with a view to attacking, but a
             heavy Rifle and Machine Gun fire
             was at once opened on them, they did
             not make a second attempt. We
             considered our success was entirely
             due to a properly organised supply
             of bombs and the steadfastness of
             the bombers. There were three
             lines of supplies organised via
             New Trench from point G.SS12 to the
             Y in St. Elie Avenue, also via
             St. Elie Avenue and via Goeben
             Avenue. We expended over 2,000
             bombs in 2½ hours.
             2nd Lt. E.H. Bentall, D Co. was
             killed during bombardment.
             2nd Lt. E.T. Beddy, C Co. was
             killed during the bombardment.

4th   The Battalion arrived and took over
             billets in the Rue-de-Brusy, Bethune
             at 5.30 a.m. During the remainder
             of the day the Battalion rested.

5th   The Battalion spent the day clear-
             ing up and refitting clothing.

6th   Brigadier General A.C. Daly came
             around Company billets at 11.30am.
             He paid the Battalion this informal
             visit and congratulated each Company
             on their excellent work from
             September 29th to October 3rd.

7th   The Battalion still resting in
             Billets.
             The Companies paraded under O.C's
             Companies for reconstruction of
             bombing and Company Training.

8th   The Companies were at the disposal
             of their O's C. "A" and "B" Coys.
             were on the range from 10 a.m. till
             noon. "C" and "D" Coys. practised
             bombing and Platoon drill.

1915   Appendix.

October

8th   At 8.30 p.m. the Battalion
(C'td.)   received orders to move at once
             to a place of readiness West of
             Beuvry on N. side of Main Road.
             This was due to the fact that the
             Germans were attacking all along
             the line from Hohenzollern to Loos.
             The Battalion moved off at 8.40pm.
             The whole Brigade assembled in a
             large ploughed field just W. of
             Beuvry on the N. of the Main Road
             and bivouacked there until 12 mid-
             night when the order came to march
             back to billets - the German attack
             having failed with heavy losses to
             them. The Battalion arrived back
             at billets about 1 a.m.
             Lt. A.E. Marshall joined from 4th
             Battn. & posted to "A" Coy.
             2 Lt. Romans from 18th (ex 13th)
             Batts posted to D. Co.

9th   The Brigade from 1 a.m. onwards
             were under 2 hours' notice to move.
             Coys were at the disposal of their
             Os. C. and continued practising -
             bombing - fire control - and Platoon
             drill from 10 a.m. to noon.
             2nd Lt. T.U.F. Wilson from 3rd Battn
             joined & was posted to C. Co.

10th   Sunday - Church Parade at noon.
             No other Parades.
             At 5 p.m. the Brigade ceased to be
             under 2 hours notice.

11th   Companies had running parade.

             BETHUNE.

12th   Battalion marched out to trenches
             near FOUQUEREUIL and practised
             blocking and consolidating them
             against bombing attacks.
             Brig. General Daly came up and
             looked at the work done.

13th   Companies at disposal of O.C. Coys.

14th   Companies at disposal of O.C. Coys.
             About 8 p.m. the Germans put some
             12 inch shells into BETHUNE, the
             majority falling near the Theatre.
             The South Staffords had some men
             knocked out but only some splinters
             fell near us.

1915   Appendix.

October   BETHUNE - HINGETTE.

15th   The Brigade was moved out of
           BETHUNE possibly in consequence
           of yesterday's shelling. The
           Battalion marched off at 7.30am.
           and proceeded to HINGETTE. Very
           poor billets and there had been
           some confusion as the South
           Staffs tried to get into our
           area.

           HINGETTE.

16th   Coys. at disposal of O.Cs Coys.

           HINGETTE - VENDIN.

17th   The Battalion moved at 8 a.m.
           to fresh billets at VENDIN, a
           much better place than HINGETTE.

           VENDIN.

18th   Church Parade in morning.
           Orders came in the afternoon
           for the Battalion to be ready to
           move at once. There had been
           very heavy artillery fire from
           the direction of VERMELLES.

19th   Companies paraded for Coy. Drill
           and instruction in bombing.

20th   Coys at disposal of O.C. Coys.

           VENDIN - BEUVRY.

21st   Battalion marched from VENDIN
           to fresh quarters at BEUVRY, still
           resting. Lieut. A.E. Marshall
           appointed A/Adjt. vice 2nd Lieut.
           C. Birkett, the latter being posted
           to "C" Coy.

           BEUVRY.

22nd   Coys exercised under Coy. Officers.
           Battalion orders announced the
           award of the Military Cross to
           2nd Lieut. L. E. Hall, and the
           D.C.M. to B/7790 L/Cpl. C.Headley.

23rd   Coys exercised under Coy. Officers.

Appendix.

1915

October
24th

NEUVRY - GUINCHY CAMBRIN POSTE FIXE.

Battalion moved into the Support Area, Section A relieving the 1st King's Regt. Headquarters at HARLEY STREET. Distribution of Battalion in Support Area was as follows:-

GUINCHY SUPPORT POINT -
2 Platoons of "D" Coy. in Keep.

CAMBRIN SUPPORT POINT -
1 Platoon of "A" Coy. in Keep &
3 Platoons in occupation.

POSTE FIXE. S.P. N. BANK -
1 Platoon of "D" Coy. in Keep.
" " N.P. N. BANK -
3 Platoons of D Coy. in occupation.
" " S.P. S. BANK -
1 Platoon of C Coy. in Keep.
" " N.P. S. BANK -
3 Platoons of "C" Coy. in occupation.

CAMBRIN VILLAGE -
2 Platoons of B Coy. and 1 of "A" in occupation.

The Battalion was occupied mostly in supplying working parties for the improvement of trenches under the direction of the R.E.

GUINCHY - CAMBRIN - POSTE FIXE.

25th

Battalion worked on improvement of its own quarters, the working parties ordered not being able to work on account of inclement weather.

26th

Battalion fully employed on working parties, every available man having to be turned out to find 2 parties of 320 men.

27th

GUINCHY.

Battalion was relieved in the Support Area by the 5th Liverpool Regt. at 2.30 p.m. and moved up to the front line trenches relieving the 1st King's Regt. about 3.30 p.m.
The distribution was:- "A" Coy. and 1 Platoon of "B" - KIDNEY WALK (excl) to HANOVER ST. (incl.) BRICKSTACK KEEP and BRICKSTACK TERRACE.
"C" Coy. HANOVER ST. (excl) to DAVIES ST. (incl.) BRICKSTACK TERRACE, LEICESTER SQ. and PETTICOAT LANE.
"D" Coy. DAVIES ST. (excl.) to CANADA and HUSTER ST.
"B" Coy. (less 1 Platoon) ESPERANTO TERRACE, PUDDING LANE, BATH ST. CABBAGE PATCH REDOUBT & LOVERS REDOUBT.

1915   Appendix.

October

27th   Capt. T.S. Dalby joined the
(C't'd.)   Battalion from ETAPLES and took
           over the duties of Second in
           Command.

28th   The first night in the trenches
           passed quietly, no hostile
           artillery fire, very little
           trench mortar and only inter-
           mittent rifle fire by snipers.
           A considerable amount of work
           was done on improvement of
           trenches. Weather on 28th very
           wet. Trenches in bad condition.
           The only casualty was No. 4433 Rfn.
           Cosford killed by sniper. (Head,
           bullet) He was killed about
           10.30 a.m. on the 28th and was
           buried in WOBURN ABBEY CEMETERY
           at 3 p.m.
           His Majesty the King inspected
           detachments of the First Army
           during the day. At this inspection
           the Battalion was represented by
           2 N.C.O's and 26 men (taken from
           the Transport) under the command
           of 2nd Lieut. Allfrey.

29th   Still in trenches. Enemy shelled
           & bombed with trench mortar.
           Four men wounded (one slightly from
           shock). Worked on improvement of
           trenches. G.O.C. First Corps
           visited the trenches.
           GUINCHY - ANNEQUIN.

30th   Relieved in Section A.2. by South
           Staffordshire Regt. about 12.30pm.
           One casualty on morning of 30th.
           Bullet graze in head. Enemy was
           on the whole inactive during this
           tour. After relief the Battalion
           marched to ANNEQUIN to billets.
           2nd Lieut. I.M. Harris joined the
           Battalion.

           ANNEQUIN.

31st   In billets at ANNEQUIN supplying
           working parties for cleaning etc.
           of trenches. Whilst one of these
           parties was waiting for the
           remainder to join them preparatory
           to marching off some of the party
           picked up a German rifle grenade
           which they took to a dug-out.
           The grenade exploded whilst the
           men were handling it and the ensuing
           casualties were :- 1 O.R. killed,
           1 died of wounds, 6 wounded.

1st BATTALION, KING'S ROYAL RIFLE CORPS.

<u>1915</u>   Appendix.

<u>October</u>

1st   Lieut. Colonel Armytage had orders to be at the Brigade office at 9 a.m. and did not return until lunch at 1 p.m. with the news that the Brigade would move at 4 p.m. and take over same trenches that we had left the previous morning. The Battalion to relieve the King's Own, and 1st King's on our left. The Battalion moved off at 4 pm. and was due to relieve at 7 p.m. but owing to an attack Hohenzollern Redoubt - the Hulloch Road was very unhealthy - and we were compelled to get into the trench by the side, and wait for some time, the relief was not completed until 11 p.m.
The night was very quiet on our front, some activity at the Dump and the Redoubt.

2nd   Quiet morning but the Germans shelled us a good bit in the afternoon, with no damage. Germans were very active with bombs and shelling in front of the Dump and Hohenzollern Redoubt all day. At 8.30 p.m. the H.L.I. on our right attacked to regain a portion of Gun Trench which had been lost. This attack was not successful but while it lasted the Germans shelled us rather unpleasantly. The rest of the night was fairly quiet, no bombing, but a good bit of sniping.

3rd   <u>Report of Operations.</u>
About 2.30 p.m. the Germans bombarded our front lines, support and communication trenches near the "Quarries" at Vermelles for about 2 hours, with 8" high explosive shells - Minenwerfers - and aerial torpedoes, paying special attention to their old observation post and Officers' dug-outs. During this time we were informed by the Royal Artillery

1915   Appendix.

October

3rd (C'td.) — that the Germans were seen massing behind their lines, so we were prepared for an attack. About 4.30 p.m. the Germans started bomb-attacks up the 2 trenches running S.W. from point G.5.D.91. This attack continued for 2½ hours during which time the Germans never gained a footing in either of our trenches. On one occasion they attempted to leave theirs, presumably with a view to attacking, but a hravy Rifle and Machine Gun fire was at once opened on them, they did not make a second attempt. We considered our success was entirely due to a properly organised supply of bombs and the steadfastness of the bombers. There were three lines of supplies organised via New Trench from point G.5912 to the V in St. Elie Avenue, also via St. Elie Avenue and via Goeben Avenue. We expended over 2,000 bombs in 2½ hours.
2nd Lt. E.H. Bentall, D Co. was killed during bombardment.
2nd Lt. K.T. Boddy, C Co. was killed during the bombardment.

4th — The Battalion arrived and took over billets in the Rue-de-Bruay, Bethune at 5.30 a.m. During the remainder of the day the Battalion rested.

5th — The Battalion spent the day cleaning up and refitting clothing.

6th — Brigadier General A.C. Daly came around Company billets at 11.30am. He paid the Battalion this informal visit and congratulated each Company on their excellent work from September 28th to October 3rd.

7th — The Battalion still resting in Billets.
The Companies paraded under O.C's Companies for reconstruction of bombing and Company Training.

8th — The Companies were at the disposal of their O's C. "A" and "B" Coys. were on the range from 10 a.m. till noon. "C" and "D" Coys. practised bombing and Platoon drill.

1915   Appendix.

October

8th (C'td.)   At 5.30 p.m. the Battalion received orders to move at once to a place of readiness West of Beuvry on N. side of Main Road. This was due to the fact that the Germans were attacking all along the line from Hohenzollern to Loos. The Battalion moved off at 6.40pm. The whole Brigade assembled in a large ploughed field just W. of Beuvry on the N. of the Main Road and bivouacked there until 12 midnight when the order came to march back to billets - the German attack having failed with heavy losses to them. The Battalion arrived back at billets about 1 a.m.
Lt. A.E. Marshall joined from 4th Battn. & posted to "A" Coy.
2 Lt. Rennan from 18th (ex 13th) Battn posted to D. Co.

9th   The Brigade from 1 a.m. onwards were under 2 hours' notice to move. Coys were at the disposal of their Os. C. and continued practising - bombing - fire control - and Platoon drill from 10 a.m. to noon.
2nd Lt. T.N.F. Wilson from 3rd Battn joined & was posted to C. Co.

10th   Sunday - Church Parade at noon.
No other Parades.
At 5 p.m. the Brigade ceased to be under 2 hours notice.

11th   Companies had running parade.

BETHUNE.

12th   Battalion marched out to trenches near FOUQUEREUIL and practised blocking and consolidating them against bombing attacks.
Brig. General Daly came up and looked at the work done.

13th   Companies at disposal of O.C. Coys.

14th   Companies at disposal of O.C. Coys.
About 5 p.m. the Germans put some 12 inch shells into BETHUNE, the majority falling near the Theatre. The South Staffords had some men knocked out but only some splinters fell near us.

1915 Appendix.

October — BETHUNE – HINGETTE.

15th — The Brigade was moved out of BETHUNE possibly in consequence of yesterday's shelling. The Battalion marched off at 7.30am. and proceeded to HINGETTE. Very poor billets and there had been some confusion as the South Staffs tried to get into our area.

HINGETTE.

16th — Coys. at disposal of O.Cs Coys.

HINGETTE – VENDIN.

17th — The Battalion moved at 8 a.m. to fresh billets at VENDIN, a much better place than HINGETTE.

VENDIN.

18th — Church Parade in morning. Orders came in the afternoon for the Battalion to be ready to move at once. There had been very heavy artillery fire from the direction of VERMELLES.

19th — Companies paraded for Coy. Drill and instruction in bombing.

20th — Coys at disposal of O.C. Coys.

VENDIN – BEUVRY.

21st — Battalion marched from VENDIN to fresh quarters at BEUVRY, still resting. Lieut. A.E. Marshall appointed A/Adjt. vice 2nd Lieut. C. Birkett, the latter being posted to "C" Coy.

BEUVRY.

22nd — Coys exercised under Coy. Officers. Battalion orders announced the award of the Military Cross to 2nd Lieut. L. E. Hall, and the D.C.M. to R/7750 L/Cpl. C.Hendley.

23rd — Coys exercised under Coy. Officers.

1915   Appendix.

October   BEUVRY - CUINCHY CAMBRIN PONTE FIXE.

24th   Battalion moved into the Support Area, Section A relieving the 1st King's Regt. Headquarters at HARLEY STREET. Distribution of Battalion in Support Area was as follows:-

CUINCHY SUPPORT POINT -
2 Platoons of "B" Coy. in Keep.

CAMBRIN SUPPORT POINT -
1 Platoon of "A" Coy. in Keep &
2 Platoons in occupation.

PONTE FIXE. S.P. N. BANK -
                1 Platoon of "D" Coy. in Keep.
"   "   S.P. N. BANK -
                3 Platoons of D Coy. in occupation.
"   "   S.P. S. BANK -
                1 Platoon of C Coy. in Keep.
"   "   S.P. S. BANK.-
                3 Platoons of "C" Coy. in occupation.

CAMBRIN VILLAGE -
2 Platoons of B Coy. and 1 of "A" in occupation.

The Battalion was occupied mostly in supplying working parties for the improvement of trenches under the direction of the R.E.

CUINCHY - CAMBRIN - PONTE FIXE.

25th   Battalion worked on improvement of its own quarters, the working parties ordered not being able to work on account of inclement weather.

26th   Battalion fully employed on working parties, every available man having to be turned out to find 2 parties of 320 men.

27th   CUINCHY.
Battalion was relieved in the Support Area by the 5th Liverpool Regt. at 2.20 p.m. and moved up to the front line trenches relieving the 1st King's Regt. about 3.30 p.m.
The distribution was:- "A" Coy. and 1 Platoon of "B" - RIDLEY WALK (excl) to HANOVER ST. (incl.) BRICKSTACK KEEP and BRICKSTACK TERRACE.
"C" Coy. HANOVER ST. (excl) to DAVIES ST. (incl.) BRICKSTACK TERRACE, LEICESTER SQ. and PETTICOAT LANE.
"D" Coy. DAVIES ST. (excl.) to CANADA and HUNTER ST.
"B" Coy. (less 1 Platoon) ESPERANTO TERRACE, PUDDING LANE, BATH ST. CABBAGE PATCH REDOUBT & LOVERS REDOUBT.

1915   Appendix.

October

27th (C'td.)   Capt. T.G. Dalby joined the Battalion from ETAPLES and took over the duties of Second in Command.

28th   The first night in the trenches passed quietly, no hostile artillery fire, very little trench mortar and only intermittent rifle fire by snipers. A considerable amount of work was done on improvement of trenches. Weather on 28th very wet. Trenches in bad condition. The only casualty was No. 4433 Rfn. Cosford killed by sniper. (Head, bullet) He was killed about 10.30 a.m. on the 28th and was buried in WOBURN ABBEY CEMETERY at 3 p.m.
His Majesty the King inspected detachments of the first Army during the day. At this inspection the Battalion was represented by 2 N.C.O's and 26 men (taken from the Transport) under the command of 2nd Lieut. Allfrey.

29th   Still in trenches. Enemy shelled & bombed with trench mortar. Four men wounded (one slightly from shock). Worked on improvement of trenches. G.O.C. First Corps visited the trenches.

CUINCHY - ANNEQUIN.

30th   Relieved in Section A.2. by South Staffordshire Regt. about 12.30pm. One casualty on morning of 30th. Bullet graze in head. Enemy was on the whole inactive during this tour. After relief the Battalion marched to ANNEQUIN to billets. 2nd Lieut. I.M. Harris joined the Battalion.

ANNEQUIN.

31st   In billets at ANNEQUIN supplying working parties for cleaning etc. of trenches. Whilst one of these parties was waiting for the remainder to join them preparatory to marching off some of the party picked up a German rifle grenade which they took to a dug-out. The grenade exploded whilst the men were handling it and the ensuing casualties were :- 1 O.R. killed, 1 died of wounds, 6 wounded.

6th Infantry Brigade.
2nd Division.

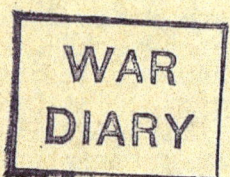

1st BATTN. THE KING'S ROYAL RIFLE CORPS.

NOVEMBER

1 9 1 5

1st Battn. The King's Royal Rifle Corps.

November 1915

In billets at ANNEQUIN.

Relieved in ANNEQUIN by South Staffordshire Regt. Marched to BETHUNE in a drenching rain and took over billets from 1st. Kings Regt.
Lieut. A.B.Bernard joined from 5th. K.R.R.
"A billet" at Bethune, the 60 yards average, with officers & training of corps whilst the Battalion was in billets on reserve.

In billets at BETHUNE. Companies at disposal of O.C.Coys. (after baths.) An interesting and useful conference of all officers presided over by C.O. on training of Companies whilst in rear in billets.
Agreed that:- (a) Snipers in each Coy. be selected & trained on definite lines.
(b) Bombing be trained for under 2nd Lieut. ____
(c) ____ entanglement training under 2nd Lieut. Potts.

1st. Annequin.
2nd. Annequin/Bethune
3rd Bethune

Army Form C. 2118.

WAR DIARY
or
INTELLIGENCE SUMMARY.
(Erase heading not required.)

1/KRR. November 1915

Instructions regarding War Diaries and Intelligence Summaries are contained in F.S. Regs., Part II. and the Staff Manual respectively. Title pages will be prepared in manuscript.

Hour, Date, Place	Summary of Events and Information	Remarks and references to Appendices
Nov 4th Bethune.	In billets at BETHUNE. Companies at disposal O.C. Coys.	
5th Bethune.	In billets BETHUNE. Companies at disposal O.C. Coys.	
6th Bethune.	In billets BETHUNE.	
7th Bethune.	In billets BETHUNE. Church parade, in unfinished Church on CHOCQUES ROAD.	
8th Bethune.	In billets BETHUNE. Programme of training (arranged at conference of 3rd.) commenced.	
9th Bethune.	In billets BETHUNE. Training programme continued.	
10th Bethune.	In billets BETHUNE. Lieut. Col. Armytage took over Temporary command of 6th Infantry Brigade during absence on leave of Brig. Gen. Daly. Capt. Dalby took over command of Battalion temporarily.	
11th Bethune.	In billets BETHUNE. Training programme continued.	

WAR DIARY
or
INTELLIGENCE SUMMARY.
(Erase heading not required.)

Army Form C. 2118.

Hour, Date, Place	Summary of Events and Information	Remarks and references to Appendices
Nov. 12th. Bethune.	In billets BETHUNE. Training programme continued	
15th. Bethune/ Annequin.	Battalion moved to FOSSE COTTAGES, ANNEQUIN, preparatory to moving to front line of trenches. Order came for Capt. Dalby to proceed on the 15th. to take command of 8th. Berkshire Regt.	
14th. Annequin/ Vermelles	Battalion took over front line of trenches between VERMELLES-LA BASSEE and VERMELLES HULLOCH ROAD (Bart Royal) just north of HOHENZOLLERN REDOUBT from 9th Fusiliers Battalion on right was Royal Berkshire Regt. and on left Welsh Fusiliers. Capt. Dalby departed to take over command of 8th Berkshire Regt. Capt. Denison took over command of Battalion. Capt. S.H Ferrand, second in Command. Casualty:- One other ranks slightly wounded in neck by shrapnel. Remained at duty.	
15th Vermelles	In trenches. The QUARRY heavily shelled between 2 and 3.30 p.m. Days casualties, two other ranks wounded, not badly	
16th Vermelles	In trenches. Quiet day. Compliments	

Army Form C. 2118.

WAR DIARY
or
INTELLIGENCE SUMMARY.
(Erase heading not required.)

Instructions regarding War Diaries and Intelligence Summaries are contained in F.S. Regs., Part II. and the Staff Manual respectively. Title pages will be prepared in manuscript.

Hour, Date, Place	Summary of Events and Information	Remarks and references to Appendices
Nov 17th Vermelles / Beuvry.	In trenches. Relieved at 1.40.p.m. by South Staffordshire Regt. 2nd. Lieut. J.W.E.Paul slightly wounded. Remained at entry. Battalion marched to BEUVRY and took over billets from 2nd. South Staffordshire Regt.	
18th Beuvry.	In billets, cleaning up. 2nd. Lieut. F.J.Chambers joined from Cadet School STOMER	
19th Beuvry.	In billets BEUVRY.	
20th Beuvry / Vermelles	Battalion moved from BEUVRY to Support Area to Y.4. and Z.0. Battalions in front 1st. Herts. in Z.0. and 1st. King's in Y.4. We relieved 1st. Herts who moved to front trenches. 7 Cadets from B spent the night under instruction.	
21st Vermelles.	In Support Area, work on trenches. Two Companies of 18th. R.F. joined for instruction. "C" and "D" Coys. went to FOSSE COTTAGES.	
22nd Vermelles	In Support Area, work on trenches. The two Coys. of R.E. went up to front line and were replaced by two Coys from the front line.	

WAR DIARY
or
INTELLIGENCE SUMMARY.
(Erase heading not required.)

Army Form C. 2118.

Instructions regarding War Diaries and Intelligence Summaries are contained in F.S. Regs., Part II. and the Staff Manual respectively. Title pages will be prepared in manuscript.

Hour, Date, Place	Summary of Events and Information	Remarks and references to Appendices
Nov. 23rd. Vermelles. Beuvry.	In Support Area, work on trenches. Two Coys. of 18th. R.F. left trenches for ANNEQUIN SOUTH. Our "A" and "B" Coys. were relieved by "C" and "D" Coys. and took over 5th. King's Regt. billets at BEUVRY.	
24th. Beuvry.	Marched out from Support Area (on orders of Brig. Genl.) at 4.25 p.m. and took over Billets at BEUVRY. The following Officers joined:- Capt. A. M. Messey, Lieut. Phillips, 2nd. Lieut. Dunkils, 2nd. Lieut. Anderson, 2nd. Lieut. Howell, 2nd. Lieut. Bellows	
25th. Beuvry.	In billets at BEUVRY.	
26th. Beuvry. Cambrin.	Relieved 1st. Berkshire Regt 2 1 1s. Bert's Regt. on our right, 1st. King's Liverpool Regt on our left.	
27th. Cambrin.	In trenches. One casualty, (one other rank wounded in head) bullet. A party of 3 Officers, 1 C.S.M and 20 N.C.O's from 22nd. R.F. visited the trenches for instructions.	
28th. Cambrin.	In trenches. A party of 3 Officers, 1 C.S.M. and 20 N.C.O's from 22nd. R.F. visited trenches for instruction as previous party marched out at about 9.15 a.m. One casualty, slight wound in neck, other ranks	

Army Form C. 2118

WAR DIARY
or
INTELLIGENCE SUMMARY.
(Erase heading not required.)

Instructions regarding War Diaries and Intelligence Summaries are contained in F.S. Regs., Part II. and the Staff Manual respectively. Title pages will be prepared in manuscript.

Hour, Date, Place	Summary of Events and Information	Remarks and references to Appendices
For 29th Cambrian	In trenches. Enemy's artillery very active. Our artillery shelled BUCY for 2 hours. 41st Coy of 22nd Bavarian Regiment commenced fire instruction. They had one casualty. Reports said to hand.	
30th Cambrian Bucy	Relieved in Sub section 2.0. by 5th King's Regt. and billeted by billets in BUCY. Our casualty, other ranks, slightly shrapnel wounded. Lieut. Col. Bury/Lys resumed command of the Battalion.	

6th Infantry Brigade.

2nd Division.

(Battn. transferred to 99th Bde. 2nd Div. 12.12.15)

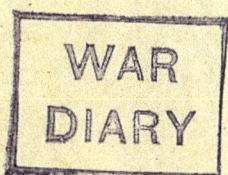

1st BATTN. THE KING'S ROYAL RIFLE CORPS.

DECEMBER

1 9 1 5
(1.12.15 - 17.12.15)

1/4KR December 1915

WAR DIARY

Dec. 1st. 1915.
Beuvry.   In billets. _____ 1/5. _____ D.C.M.
                 _____ 30/11/15.

" 2nd "
Beuvry.   In billets.

" 3rd "
Beuvry.   In billets. Major Vernon arrived and took over 2nd in Command.
                 8 Shells (light) dropped in BEUVRY.

" 4th "
Trenches.   Relieved R.Berks.Regt. in Sub-section #2.2. (CAMBRIN SUPPORT
                 POINT). _____ 2nd Lieut. _____
                 _____ Casualty, 1 O.R. killed bullet in
                 stomach.

" 5th "
Trenches.   Trenches. Cleaning up very bad trenches. Casualties, 1 O.R.
                 killed; 2 O.R. wounded.

" 6th "
Trenches.   Trenches. Still cleaning up. Casualties nil.

" 7th "
Beuvry.   Relieved by 5th King's Regt. Marched to billets at BEUVRY.
                 Casualties, 1 O.R. killed 2 wounded by German Rifle Grenade.

WAR DIARY

Dec. 8th 1915.
Beuvry.   In billets at BEUVRY.

" 9th "
Beuvry.   In billets at BEUVRY.

" 10th "
Trenches.   Marched to relieve 1st R. Berks. Regt. in 21. "D" "B" and "C"
                 Coys. in front line. No casualties. Trenches in very bad
                 state.

" 11th "
Trenches.   In 21. Working hard on trenches. No casualties.

" 12th "
Trenches.   In 21 working hard on trenches. Casualties, 1 O.R. 17th
                 Middlesex Regt. Killed.

WAR DIARY.

Dec. 13, 1916. Relieved in Z.1. by 5th King's Regt. Marched to billets in BEUVRY.

14th Beuvry. In billets at BEUVRY.

15th Beuvry. In billets at BEUVRY.

16th Beuvry. In billets at BEUVRY. This being our last night in the 6th Bde. General Daly dined with us and we all spent a very pleasant evening. During the course of the evening the Colonel in a short speech expressed the deep regret of all of us at having to leave the 6th Bde. where we had all been very happy, owing in a very great measure to the consideration shown at all times to all ranks by the Brigadier and his staff, and to the spirit of camaraderie and general good feeling which existed throughout the whole Brigade. In acknowledging the compliment, the Brigadier shared our regrets at the parting and expressed his appreciation of the help which the Battalion had always given to the Brigade. He stated that he could claim very long connexion with the 60th for it through his father, claim very long connexion with the 60th for it was nearly 60 years ago that his father wrote from India during the Mutiny to say that "that splendid Regiment the 60th" had arrived to his assistance.

17th Beuvry. "A" and "C" Coys. moved to Z.1. trenches relieving 5th King's Regt. On our right 22nd Fusiliers; on our left 1st R. Berks. Regt. 9.a.m.
"B" and "D" Coys. moved to billets at BETHUNE (nr Tobacco Factory) 11.a.m.
A minor operation planned for the purpose of obtaining information from the Enemy's trenches was postponed owing to the weather conditions being unfavourable. Casualties nil.

1 Herts Regt

Feb 1916

Vol XV

G.H.Q. Troops
on Feb 20th